CASE STUDIES OF SECURITY PROBLEMS AND THEIR SOLUTIONS

Studies in Health Technology and Informatics

Editors

Volume 75

Previously published in this series

Vol. 45. J. Dudeck, B. Blobel, W. Lordieck and T. Bürkle (Eds.), New Technologies in Hospital Information Systems
Vol. 46. U. Gerdin, M. Tallberg and P. Wainwright (Eds.), Nursing Informatics
Vol. 47. W. Ceusters, P. Spyns, G. De Moor and W. Martin (Eds.), Syntactic-Semantic Tagging of Medical Texts: The Multi-TALE Project
Vol. 48. J. Graafmans, V. Taipale and N. Charness (Eds.), Gerontechnology
Vol. 49. L. van den Broek and A.J. Sikkel (Eds.), Health Cards '97
Vol. 50. J.D. Westwood, H.M. Hoffman, D. Stredney and S.J. Weghorst (Eds.), Medicine Meets Virtual Reality
Vol. 51. J. Mantas (Ed.), Advances in Health Telematics Education
Vol. 52. B. Cesnik, A.T. McCray and J.-R. Scherrer (Eds.), MedInfo '98
Vol. 53. M.C. Sievert, D.E. Moxley, N.J. Ogg and T.B. Patrick, Thesaurus of Health Informatics
Vol. 54. O. Ferrer-Roca and M. Sosa-Iudicissa (Eds.), Handbook of Telemedicine
Vol. 55. H.M.J. Goldschmidt, M.J.T. Cox, R.J.E. Grouls, W.A.J.H. van de Laar and G.G. van Merode, Reference Information Model for Clinical Laboratories
Vol. 56. I. Iakovidis, S. Maglavera and A. Trakatellis (Eds.), User Acceptance of Health Telematics Applications
Vol. 57. J. Mantas (Ed.), Health and Medical Informatics Education in Europe
Vol. 58. G. Riva, B.K. Wiederhold and E. Molinari (Eds.), Virtual Environments in Clinical Psychology and Neuroscience
Vol. 59. I.A.F. Stokes (Ed.), Research into Spinal Deformities 2
Vol. 60. M. Di Rienzo, G. Mancia, G. Parati, A. Pedotti and A. Zanchetti (Eds.), Methodology and Clinical Applications of Blood Pressure and Heart Rate Analysis
Vol. 61. R.A. Mortensen (Ed.), ICNP® and Telematic Applications for Nurses in Europe
Vol. 62. J.D. Westwood, H.M. Hoffman, R.A. Robb and D. Stredney (Eds.), Medicine Meets Virtual Reality
Vol. 63. R. Rogers and J. Reardon, Recommendations for International Action
Vol. 64. M. Nerlich and R. Kretschmer (Eds.), The Impact of Telemedicine on Health Care Management
Vol. 65. In production
Vol. 66. In production
Vol. 67. J. Oates and H. Bjerregaard Jensen (Eds.), Building Regional Health Care Networks in Europe
Vol. 68. P. Kokol, B. Zupan, J. Stare, M. Premik and R. Engelbrecht (Eds.), Medical Informatics Europe '99
Vol. 69. In production
Vol. 70. J.D. Westwood, H.M. Hoffman, G.T. Mogel, R.A. Robb and D. Stredney (Eds.), Medicine Meets Virtual Reality 2000
Vol. 71. J.T. Ottesen and M. Danielsen (Eds.), Mathematical Modelling in Medicine
Vol. 72. I. Iakovidis, S. Maglavera and A. Trakatellis (Eds.), User Acceptance of Health Telematics Applications
Vol. 73. W. Sermeus, N. Kearney, J. Kinnunen, L. Goossens and M. Miller (Eds.), WISECARE. Workflow Information Systems for European Nursing Care
Vol. 74. O. Rienhoff, C. Laske, P. van Eecke, P. Wenzlaff and U. Piccolo (Eds.), A Legal Framework for Security in European Health Telematics.

ISSN: 0926-9630

Case Studies of Security Problems and their Solutions

Edited by

Gunnar O. Klein

Centre for Health Telematics, Karolinska Institute, Stockholm, Sweden

IOS Press

Ohmsha

Amsterdam • Berlin • Oxford • Tokyo • Washington, DC

ISBN 1 58603 050 7 (IOS Press)
ISBN 4 274 90372 9 C3047 (Ohmsha)
Library of Congress Catalog Card Number: 00-103715

Publisher
IOS Press
Nieuwe Hemweg 6B
1013 BG Amsterdam
The Netherlands
fax: +31 20 620 3419
e-mail: order@iospress.nl

Distributor in the UK and Ireland
IOS Press/Lavis Marketing
73 Lime Walk
Headington
Oxford OX3 7AD
England
fax: +44 1865 75 0079

Distributor in the USA and Canada
IOS Press, Inc.
5795-G Burke Centre Parkway
Burke, VA 22015
USA
fax: +1 703 323 3668
e-mail: iosbooks@iospress.com

Distributor in Germany
IOS Press
Spandauer Strasse 2
D-10178 Berlin
Germany
fax: +49 30 242 3113

Distributor in Japan
Ohmsha, Ltd.
3-1 Kanda Nishiki-cho
Chiyoda-ku, Tokyo 101
Japan
fax: +81 3 3233 2426

PRINTED IN THE NETHERLANDS

Contents

1. Introduction

Gunnar O. Klein

1.1 The SIREN project

The scope of this accompanying measure to the Health Telematics Programme of the European Commission is to assist health care provider groups using regional health care networks to establish necessary security services. The activity concerned primarily the regional health care network projects within the EU programme but also targeted other regional and national user groups operating or planning for health care networks. The project has collected experiences from major regional health care networks throughout Europe with regard to security problems. Using these experiences and security expertise, particularly from the TrustHealth project of the programme, SIREN is disseminating information on good examples of solutions to the user groups. In addition to this booklet, the SIREN project has conducted a series of workshops and conference presentations in different European countries.

SIREN also provided educational material to highlight the problems and point at state of the art solutions available through the world wide web server: www.ehto.be/projects/siren

The project will also provide directed implementation assistance to a few health telematics projects that are looking to put the security services developed within the TrustHealth project on trial.

1.2 Scope of this booklet

This chapter provides an introduction to the problem area of securing communication in large health telematics networks. Chapter 2 describes the challenges with regard to legal requirements on digital data, particularly with regard to issues of proving authenticity. Chapter 3 provides an overview of typical healthcare applications and highlights some of the different security requirements posed. The major part of this booklet provides reports from security analyses and selected solutions from a number of different environments, mainly taken from European projects with participants from many different countries.

At the end of the booklet the SIREN project provides a summary of experiences and gives a series of recommendations for healthcare organisations in moving into the next millenium of secure health telematics.

1.3 The Security challenges

European healthcare is connecting ....

Information systems resources are being hooked up in ever increasing networks:

- Within healthcare establishments
- In a regional collaboration between different organisations
- In some countries a national healthcare network is established and we even see some cross border communication of health data although it is in its infancy.

Here are some examples of healthcare networks that are currently in use or being planned on a large scale in the near future:

- Prescriptions for medical drugs and ordering of supplies from hospital pharmacies
- Laboratory requests and results sent via EDI
- Invoices from health care establishments to payment bodies
- Transfer of multimedia medical records for use in remote specialist consultation

However, it is not enough to be able to send millions of bytes at low cost. There are a number of important security aspects that call for attention where we need to meet the increasing challenges

1.3.1 How can we meet the increasing challenges

- **Legislation**

E.g. the Data Protection Directive that should have been implemented in all member states on October 24 1998.The Draft Directive on Electronic Signatures (issued May 1998 and likely to be approved in a revised form April 1999).

- **Business requirements**

New ways of organising healthcare with new paths of collaborative work between different healthcare establishments connected electronically

- **Concerned patients**

The patients demand professional protection of "their" important and sensitive information. In a near future will Patients directly access health information systems, e.g. through Internet connected home PCs.

1.3.2 The key issues

- How can we protect patient privacy?

- How can we ensure legal accountability of medical professionals and administrative staff? How can we provide an equivalent of a signature in ink on important health documents when these are communicated between systems.

1.3.3 The legal analysis

Siren has collected a number of legal experts to provide expert advice on the current situation with regard to such issues as how can we use electronic documents as evidence. SIREN analyses the new EU initiative to create a common legislation for electronic signatures and its relation to various national situations with healthcare specific laws.

There are a number of issues to consider in relation to the legal situation of health telematics. SIREN is focusing on the problems of document authenticity and accountability of the professionals handling digital information. Moving to handling of digital data and connecting various information systems creates many different new situations that are poorly catered for in the current legal systems. In many cases, however, the traditional legal treatment is still valid for the digital world but needs some new thinking in interpreting the issues. Some of the traditional problems that ended in courts will still be very valid but take slightly different forms and must not be overlooked — for example:

- The risk of forgery

  A patient may gain benefits from forging some health information, to pretend there is no medical problem when there is or falsely showing a condition that may render some financial benefits.

  A healthcare professional may forge health date for instance to alter the judgement of a possible malpractice case. There is also a clear risk of forgery for direct financial benefits showing evidence of treatments to payment bodies that never took place.

When using digital documents with ones and zeroes without any characteristic as appearing in original form, many of the traditional ways of detecting and proving forgery has disappeared. These issues have rather recently gained proper attention of the legislators but still most countries do not have a proper legislation to handle this.

A European initiative has been taken by the Commission that has issued a draft directive on Electronic Signatures.

http://europa.eu.int/comm/dg15/en/media/infso/sign.htm

Siren has conducted a workshop to study this and other legal issues. A particular healthcare problem is where special laws give formal requirements on documents such as prescriptions which have to be on special paper forms and be duly signed (in a form interpreted by the courts to be in ink!)

Please consider the SIREN deliverable:

D4.2: *Report of the 2nd SIREN legal workshop — Legal Issues of Health Telematics Networks* which also contains many references to other work.

1.3.4 Some core techniques

The SIREN accompanying measure has been selecting some core requirements for security services and techniques to meet these. The further background to this analysis was documented during the Infosec project Trusted Health Information Systems, final reports of which are available from Spri and the TrustHealth 1 project.

One of the core security services for achieving both confidentiality and accountability is a secure user authentication. In order for access control systems to work properly in granting access rights to authorised users it is essential to have high assurance in the method for user authentication. It is a key function to achieve a secure identification of professional users of telematic services, electronic records but in the future we will need it also for patients as users of health information systems. Password protection simply is not good enough for the modern networking environment. Instead one should use:

- Secure user authentication based on cryptographic smart cards, from the PC work station to local and remote servers. This is also an important issue to allow a minimum of administration when many users make use of several different systems perhaps even controlled by different organisations. SIREN can provide information about state of the art techniques using smart cards and cryptographic authentication.

- Digital signatures

  The activity will use the experiences and services developed within the TrustHealth project for cryptographic security services supporting user authentication as well as digital signatures and confidentiality protection.

- Confidentitality protection using encryption

  SIREN can provide advice on what algorithms and protocols to use. This is both an issue of basic cryptographic functions but also of linking the cryptographic techniques in a proper way to communication protocols for securing data objects for messaging or for the creation of secure data channels, e.g. for confidentiality protected web access.

- A supporting infrastructure with Certification Service Providers

  This is an issue of strong importance where the healthcare sector must ensure that its demands are met for national as well as cross border communication. A special issue is how to provide an electronic proof of professional registration as a physician, pharmacist, nurse etc.

- Security management

  The experiences from the ISHTAR project on security guidelines will also be channeled through this activity as relevant to the regional networking.

1.3.4.1 Public key cryptography and its infrastructure

A major boost of interest for cryptographic techniques has come with the advent of asymmetric cryptographic methods in a variety of ways to achieve the key security aspects data integrity and confidentiality. In this paradigm every user of the health care information system should be equipped with a personal authentication and signature device that contains a private key and a cryptographic engine in the form of a chip on a smart card. Although the mathematical foundation has been known for more than 20 years, it has only recently been possible to implement these principles at a reasonably low cost and with appropriate security.

An infrastructure of Trusted Third Party organisations must be established with the major function of certifying the linkage between the identity of an individual (or an organisation) and its associated public key. The asymmetric system allows verification of signatures created with private keys to be carried out with the corresponding public key component. This does not need to be kept secret but could be widely distributed to communicating partners and made available in public directory services. It can also be used to encrypt messages that can only be decrypted and read by the user with the corresponding private key.

The directory services for public key certificates will most often be based on the X.500/X.509 standards and will in that project mainly used for security services. However, the same resource can be very valuable also as a source of other information, mainly the electronic and other addresses of health care parties.

The TrustHealth 1 consortium developed a set of common publicly available interfaces to allow interoperability between different products. Only relatively modest development efforts are necessary to align Application Programming Interfaces, document and package tool-kits for application integration.

However, even if the TrustHealth project also developed guidelines on how to understand and use the interface specifications, there is a great need for training and support for real implementations to stimulate the rapid uptake of these important techniques. The first step is to create broad awareness about the problems and the available solutions to everybody involved in strategic planning of health telematics networks.

A major new development and experience to be gained during the TrustHealth project is the establishment of a network of Trusted Third Party Services. Today there are no such organisations in routine use in any sector although several trials are ongoing and similar functions are performed within certain large organisations such as banks.

Technical systems with high security, properly evaluated by independent parties, and with appropriate operating procedures in specially protected environments, are necessary. At the same time great care must be taken to ensure that a high degree of service to the user community can be given and that costs can be held at an acceptable level.

It is important to bear in mind that the health sector has certain characteristics that create special demand for such TTP-services. One aspect that will be explored during the trials is the association of registration as a health care professional in addition to the core identity registration of users common with all sectors. The aspects of requirements to handle access to patient data cards by professionals also create special quite complicated problems. The requirement for trans-European interoperability in the health sector is also stronger than in many other areas, partly dictated by the needs to handle the free movement of people (the patients) across borders with the associated requirement to provide medical attention outside the home region.

The infrastructure of Trusted Third Parties (TTPs) will perform the following services:

- Generation of cryptographic keys and issuing of personal smart cards to the users
- Creation of digitally signed public key certificates linking a public key to the identity of the user
- On-line directory services according to the X.500 standards with certificates and addresses

Trusthealth 2 is developing and will operate TTPs, based on nationally trustworthy organisations related to the health care sector, linked in a pan-European network through the participating telecom operators. These TTP services will provide an important resource for European health care, professionals, industry, European and National telematics projects and patients.

This book is intended to provide an insight into current experience with security in healthcare networks. It can be used as an introduction with many links to further information, as a reference to some of the most important EU funded projects of the fourth framework where security issues were treated, and using the summary and concluding recommendations as a guide to compare with the security strategy of any large healthcare organisation.

The Siren project hopes that the reader will find it useful and informative.

2. The Legal Challenges

Per Furberg and Gunnar O. Klein

2.1 Abstract

When information systems and networks are replacing traditional document procedures, archiving and postal services in the healthcare sector, insecure routines may be avoided by elaborating appropriate procedures and technical protection measures.

These routines need to be supported by the legal system to create public confidence in digital documents with digital signatures and related services. Instead of a completely new legal framework, at the risk of forgetting certain issues or having to invent the wheel again, existing legal principles should be utilised and — when necessary — adapted to new patterns of action. Such a starting point may create a base for legally unified regulations of paper-based and electronic routines, with security maintained. By adapting the definition of document and the well known procedures regarding e.g. archiving and postal services to the electronic environment it will become natural for the solution of various legal questions to be taken from those rules which are already established for paper documents.

This chapter focuses on the legal requirements on electronic document management including the possibility of using them as evidence. It does not go into detail on the equally important but more well-known requirements for confidentiality based on special healthcare legislation and protection of the rights of the data subject as provided for in the "Data Protection Directive" 95/46/EC.

2.2 Healthcare information management

The relatively few actions possible with well established routines for the traditional paper based information management might seem to be replaced by nearly limitless options when information systems and electronic networks are introduced. This section attempts to give a brief description of the major types of information management in healthcare relevant for communication projects. It by no means attempts to cover everything but focuses on typical use relevant in all healthcare systems and which represents large volumes.

The following descriptions are based on functional characteristics and as much as possible make relevant analogies to traditional routines.

2.2.1 Creating clinical documents

Such documents describe

- some aspect or all of the clinical condition of the patient,
- the care (including examinations) given, and
- the care planned.

There is always at least one (sometimes two) responsible persons, usually registered healthcare professionals of some sort, that writes or by his/her name and often signature takes responsibility for the recorded fact that may be based on more or less subjective or objective primary data.

These clinical documents may have different purposes and often there is a combination of at least these:

- Accountability — to document the situation for reasons of possible unlikely need to control professional action. There is often special Medical record legislation in the member states that makes this mandatory for professionals but it is always considered good practice.
- To guide the further care given at the same healthcare entity — even if it is a single doctor's office the doctor may need the memory support of a document. But it is more often a way of communicating between care team members within an organisation.
- To guide the further care given by other entities — in this case the document is intended to be communicated outside of its primary creation site. Examples are referrals and prescriptions of medicine.
- To be the basis for financial accounting and possibly invoicing.
- To be used in current or future clinical research.

Please note that medical or healthcare records that are sometimes referred to as documents normally are better looked upon as a collection of documents where each entry, from a few lines to several pages with a specific author and time point, is considered as a separate document. The following main characteristics of a clinical document may be mentioned.

- a named issuer (originator) of the document,
- a signature to be able to authenticate issuer and original content,
- a clearly defined content (delineation of start and end with features that provide proof of data integrity), and
- a time of issue.

2.2.2 Communication of clinical documents

The second major information management type is the directed communication of clinical documents. The dominating situation being that one entity (often the issuer but not always) decides to send a document to another entity. In addition to the basic characteristics of a document as listed above the following characteristics become important:

- sender
- recipient
- recipient address
- time of transmission, and
- proof of receipt (or delivery).

Please note that in the situations where the document is a bearer instrument additional transactions may need to be implemented to match the functionality of the original paper document as carrier of a certain right. One example is as a prescription for medication, which entitles the holder to have one and only one filling.

2.2.3 Administrative documents

There are a number of administrative documents within and between healthcare organisations. Most of these are no different from what is being handled in other sectors. A major application for communication also across borders is for invoicing or insurance claims.

There is in some situations the need for authentication, not only of the issuer of the invoice, but in addition of the patient (subject of care) and the professional incurring the cost. An attached clinical document is sometimes used as a record of the service performed making the difference between clinical and administrative data less sharp.

2.2.4 Creation of technical recordings

In healthcare there are a number of situations where instruments record data about a patient. These recordings are legally to be considered separate from documents because they are "issued" by a machine. Examples are ECG and EEG registrations, digital x-ray and ultrasound images. Although a responsible person (doctor, nurse or technician) will in most cases also produce a document regarding the specific recording, where they certify certain facts such as the identity of the patient, the settings of the instrument etc, the primary digital information comes from a state of the external physical world as detected by some electronic signal and registered by the machine. A human subject can not in most cases intelligently examine the digital recording in detail.

Such a recording of digital data could be attributed to a device and be referenced by or be a part of a document, but the technical recording should not be considered as a document per se. As major characteristics of a technical recording — which differ from a document — the following are worth mentioning:

- The digital data should be attributed to an identified signal registration and recording device, not to a person as the issuer.
- There is often no need for authentication data (that can enable a user to validate its authenticity) within the recording since a document will associate the recording with such authentication data but there may be a machine generated sequence number.
- Data integrity and various technical parameters are at focus, to ensure correct interpretation of data.

2.2.5 Information Databases or Registers

A third type of information management apart from documents and technical recordings are the Information databases that for this discussion will be called Registers. These are common in healthcare primarily for administrative purposes but sometimes also for clinical information.

Some registers are merely supporting the access to collections of documents where the focus of interest with regard to authenticity is the individually stored documents. The register contains a journal of all entries to make it possible to identify and retrieve a certain document. A healthcare record can be regarded as a good example of this.

There are however also important issues regarding the availability of the individual documents. Is the collection complete or is something missing (perhaps by a malicious action)? Therefore the register, e.g. the record file may also need authentication as such.

In the paper world there may be a specific person assigned to be responsible for the register such as the archive personnel for records in large hospitals. In the electronic world these functions are usually carried out more or less satisfactorily by the technical system, operating system protection, database manager design and specific register program design and control mechanisms.

There are also registers which are not collection of documents but where the totality of the information is something an organisation is responsible for. There may often be no possibility of tracing the source of individual records or data fields of such information Registers and perhaps not the need either. The issues of our concern are not so much the existence of the register as such but how information can be verified that is communicated from such a register.

In the paper world, the outside users of register data rely on the fact that the source of the information from a register can often be verified with some degree of certainty, although the actual information written contain no authentication characteristics typical of a document. There is often no person in charge visible, nor any signature or special letterhead paper.

In the electronic world the corresponding trust historically came from a specific electronic address, that was part of a more or less private network under some sort of control, but also based on the fact that it was technically infeasible for somebody to produce a fake register to a specific application. Today with open networks, particularly Internet, and the readily available and inexpensive database tools, this assumption is often not enough.

There are several technical possibilities to secure authentication of the connection, but there is also the possibility — to date very little explored — to have the register produce a properly protected document as an excerpt of the register, every time some piece of information is needed. That would then have proper data integrity and authentication information, probably in the form of a digital signature in combination with a statement that the document is a correct excerpt of the register.

The signatory may be a responsible clerk at the register organisation or it may be a key managed by the organisation in which case this has been proposed to be called a digital stamp, in analogy with the paper world where stamps or seals were often used by organisations to provide sufficient proof of authenticity to documents that were in fact excerpts of registers.

Registers may thus be of two types with the following characteristics:

- A collection of documents which contain their own authentication information in the form of signatures (digital signatures for electronic documents)
- In addition such registers normally contains a list of all documents registered
    - ⇒ In addition such registers normally contain a list of all documents registered and ensure that it is complete and updated within its domain.
    - ⇒ Copies of the registered documents may be communicated with no extra authentication needed

- A collection of information from which "potential" excerpts may be produced by computer programs
  - ⇒ An organisation is normally responsible for the data of a register as a whole
  - ⇒ The excerpts of information can be made available on paper or made available through data communication
  - ⇒ The register system should add authentication information to the excerpts. This may take the form of generating on demand a signed document, based on the registered information. The signature may be by an officer or by the organisation (a digital stamp).
  - ⇒ Authentication of the connection to the register and the establishment of a secure channel is another possibility

2.2.6 Document management

In addition to the problems regarding creation of digital documents and authentication of these, there are issues regarding management of documents that are not healthcare specific.

These deal with:

- storage (short and long term),
- handling incoming documents, and
- handling distribution of documents.

2.3 Legal issues

This section provides an overview of the principal problems and solutions regarding authenticity of documents and integrity of technical recordings and registers with regard to healthcare information management as described above. The following is a non-exhaustive list:

- What legal provisions are required for defining a digital document and requirements for data integrity check and authentication of issuer
- What are the problems regarding Technical Recordings
- What are the problems regarding Registers
- What are the legal issues regarding document management, storing, incoming and distribution
- What legal provisions are necessary to regulate the security techniques to be used for document and signature management and a supporting public key infrastructure

2.3.1 Documents

2.3.1.1 Traditional proceedings

The concept document gives basic mechanisms for the traditional information management. The concept has a long tradition and is normally easy to describe. The ultimate concern is the need to replace direct communication, with indirect communication, in a manner that will ascertain that the contents are originating from the designated issuer, though he is not present. Such documents are signed, sorted into files or divided into units of a similar kind and also noted in a diary, in a registrar's office when less demanding measures are insufficient.

When a misuse is directed towards the functions of a traditional document, legal protection is normally provided in criminal law, mainly as forgery (in a broad sense). These provisions reflect the general view on secure information management.

2.3.1.2 Different kinds of forgery

Legal doctrine has elaborated a classification of different kinds of falsification. This grouping is normally not addressed as a whole in the legal systems, but is in accordance with the penal codes in most European countries and provides a helpful overview.

Material falsification includes methods of procedure where the document is not produced, in whole or in part; by the person who appears to be the originator, e.g. unlawfully writing another person's signature on a contract.[1] *Immaterial falsification* means an attack on the functioning of a document, while the object is left unaffected, e.g. to deny ones' signature on a contract.[2]

It may seem remarkable that a discussion concerning electronic information management would have bearing upon criminal law. However, laws and regulations in other areas are built on the presumption that the fundamental functions and parameters of existing traditional information management are given factors. Remaining provisions are mainly intended to differentiate between levels of protection within these given frames; e.g. demands of written, signed and possibly also certified documents. It is interesting to see how mainly the same need for protection will arise in the electronic environment.

2.3.1.3 Changes when these legal concepts are confronted with IT

The traditional and in principle uniform concept document has in the IT-environment changed into a more divided meaning. It is necessary to make a distinction between

- *digital documents*; i.e. running text signed in electronic form, and
- *databases/registers*; i.e. structured information concerning certain facts, as described above

1 *Positive material falsification* consists of actions whereby a false document is produced (e.g. to sign a contract with another persons name) or utilised (e.g. the usage of a manipulated identity card). *Negative material falsification* means that an authentic document is destroyed completely or in part (e.g. destruction of a contract).

2 *Positive immaterial falsification* might consist of so-called *intellectual* forgery, that is the production of an authentic document with an untrue content (e.g. to issue a certificate with an erroneous statement). It might also consist of a misuse of an authentic and true document by someone in order to verify something other than what is intended to be proven by that document (e.g. to use another persons identity card while impersonating that person). *Negative immaterial falsification* means to hinder an authentic and true document from fulfilling the functions it is meant for, without a material attack (e.g. denial of signature).

2.3.1.4 A legally unified regulation

The traditional management of paper documents may be replaced by digitally signed documents and related services. Instead of creating a completely new legal framework existing achievements should be utilised and adapted to new patterns of action in the IT environment. Thus, there is a need for a definition of digital document. With such a definition it will become natural for the solution of various legal questions to be taken from those rules which are already established for paper documents.

Consequently, the traditional management of paper documents may be replaced by signed digital documents, with the security maintained. This will create a base for legally unified regulations of paper-based and electronic routines, with security maintained.

2.3.2 Protection of closed places and sealed packages/envelopes

2.3.2.1 The basic routines

Traditional documents are kept in offices, archives and other *closed places of storage.* When the documents are *sent by mail,* they are distributed in sealed envelopes and forwarded by reliable modes of transportation, guarding against unauthorised access, damage etc. An establishment's mail opening procedures are arranged according to well-established routine, and the notification of a certain establishment's address normally leaves no room for doubt. The personnel are familiar with these protective measures, which provides a functioning social control and thus a secure environment.

This *physical protection* of information will hardly need to be described. This is true also when medical records are forwarded between wards and hospitals or in connection with the treatment of a patient. Proceedings have been elaborated to safeguard that the information is available only in due course and is protected from damage.

Ultimately the issue is to *replace the human guarding of objects, with a physical or logical defence*, in a manner that will ascertain that the information independent of whether it at present is in storage or, being transmitted or received is

- protected from unauthorised access (independent of whether it at present is in storage or being transmitted or received),
- protected from destruction, and
- available in readable form, whenever necessary.

There is also a need for alternatives that allow for the possibility — when information is directly communicated — to *immediately clarify* e.g. that it has reached the addressee.

2.3.2.2 Legal protection concerning rooms, places and communication

These routines are supported by the legal system. In the case of misuse directed towards the basic functions of traditional information management, fundamental legal protection — in this field as well — is provided in criminal law. We can benefit in the IT-environment from this carefully considered legal protection. Administrative regulations for certain areas, giving special provisions adapted to the routines in question, should be observed as well.

To protect against encroachment upon privacy, most countries have enacted provisions in their criminal code against unlawful intrusion, breach of domicilary, intrusion in safe depositories and the like. In other provisions a corresponding protection is given, regarding certain places or objects kept safely, under seal or lock or otherwise enclosed, for the purpose of e.g. state security, trade and industry. For many years there have also existed provisions concerning the protection of traditional telephone calls.

This protection of traditional structures is stable and well known, and procedures in the healthcare sector have for a long time been adapted to this environment. Existing achievements should be utilised rather than creating a completely new legal framework. Otherwise we will run the risk of forgetting certain issues or of being thrown back to square one.

2.3.2.2.1 Legal changes — protection of information versus sealed places and packages

Most European countries have enacted new provisions concerning e.g. unlawfully procured access or alteration of data.[3] Furthermore, procedural law has been analysed with regard to the use of search and seizure and technical surveillance for the purpose of criminal investigations, such as interception of telecommunications.[4]

This work has clearly shown a gliding from the protection of certain places towards regulations aimed directly at the protection of certain information; cf. regulations concerning unlawful intrusion in e.g. an office with provisions regarding breach of professional secrecy, copyright or other (immaterial) rights. For example, it is normally not criminalised to read a (private) paper document on someone else's desk if the entrance is lawful — the protection is spatial — whereas unlawful access to data itself is made an offence, independent of whether or not the intruder is unauthorised to access other documents in the same electronic space, e.g. a certain folder on a hard disc.

Progress in the IT-environment has however showed that the lack of traditional physical borderlines more and more has been replaced by logical protection in the IT-environment. A continued transition from traditional protected rooms and places to corresponding electronic entities in an open IT-environment requires such protection at every health care establishment and ward. Consequently, every electronic archive belonging to a certain health care provider should be placed on an equal footing with a room at the establishment, independent of where the electronic storage physically takes place.

It is true that criminal law establishes such basic borders. However, difficulties appear as a consequence of the usually *poorly considered practical handling* of who is allowed to access where and to what. Such terms as "unlawfully" are clear enough to distinguish allowed access from forbidden entrance in the traditional environment terms. Regulations for certain areas are given the necessary supplemental provisions. The process of maturing in the IT-environment has unfortunately not yet created the necessary conditions for such clear borders.

Corresponding issues arise in the context of European telematics services. Paper based routines are built on existing and widely accepted procedures of liability and risk together with routines and regulations adapted to the traditional patterns of, for example, rooms, closed places of storage, envelopes etc. The prerequisites for protection of

---

[3] Cf. the Council of Europe Recommendation No. R (89) 9 on computer-related crime and the final report of the European Committee on Criminal Problems.

[4] Cf. the Council of Europe Recommendation No. R (95) 13 on problems of criminal procedural law connected with information technology and the explanatory memorandum.

information in this area are completely changed by the quasi-material character of data. Fundamental questions are further tied to *new parties and new infrastructures* in computerised patterns of administration, commerce, transport, etc. Will it e.g. be possible to prove who has caused loss by hindering certain messages or digital functions? Another example is the question arising from errors in automatically generated transactions. Who will be responsible for errors made either mistakenly or deliberately?

Consequently we need clear distinctions between:

- **personal electronic storage space, such as private e-mail areas and the like; comparable to the professionals wardrobe or the locked drawer in his desk**
- **different health care authorities electronic archives**
- **different actors and their responsibilities in the new infrastructure.**

2.3.3 The traditional paper document — a further analysis

A *paper document* normally consists of three aspects:

1. the carrier (the sheet of paper)
2. text and pictures (the physical representation of the information)
3. information about the originator to verify the authenticity (usually a written signature).

These aspects are often seen as material/physical. The connections among carrier, text and signature are self-evident. Therefore normally only the carrier (the paper) is mentioned. It provides parameters and structure to one finalised representation of the content. These aspects are physically "locked" via the paper that carries the information in one "unchangeable" combination.

2.3.4 The electronic document — new dimensions

The new *IT*-dimensions concerning documents could be summarised as follows.

Paper documents are *material* objects, things, while digitally represented information from a traditional point of view may not be described as a physical object. In a paper document the connections among carrier, text and signature are self-evident. Therefore normally only the carrier (the paper) is mentioned. It gives delimitation and structure to one finalised representation of the content.

Electronic documents confer new dimensions. Descriptions of electronic documents will normally make immaterial wordings, not physical objects, the starting point. It could on occasion be difficult to obtain information about how the user intended to process-stored text-data and computer programs.

In a paper document the text and the signature aspects are physically "locked" via the paper that carries the information in one "unchangeable" and durable combination. There is *no such "lock" for the information* in an electronic document without certain technical authentication procedures. The fixed and "locked" state in a paper document is, in the IT-environment, replaced by the possibility to process the data into a variety of constellations (potential documents).[5]

Paper documents are in principle *unique physical examples*; originals. Every paper document to a certain degree contains a unique physical character as object, often given by the written signature. Data are not unique as physical examples. The unique existence of IT material is built upon the storing and transmission of original *contents*. An IT stored record has no other unique character than those bound to the pattern of digits.

A paper document may, as a physical example, be in a person's *possession*, thereby establishing legal rights. The paper is the physical carrier of certain right. This function is normally not possible to recreate in the IT-environment where, for example, a data transmission results in the multiplying of the digital bits and not the physical transference of a physical example. The legal functions built into a certain physical object are in the IT-environment normally substituted by *registration* in a database.

In a paper document *the stored state and the readable state* are identical. The paper document is immediately readable and the storing is normally in a language that the user will understand without special training, the opposite of digital documents that must be transformed to a recognisable format for human scrutiny.

Consequently, a manipulation of a paper document has to be a *material attack*, traceable upon the physical object. An individual makes — often unconsciously — a visual authenticity-control when he is reading an important paper document. A manipulation of a digital record consists of *untraceable alterations of a bit pattern* which may be manipulated during the transferral among different states and media. The visual authenticity control of a paper document has no correspondent in the IT-area[6] and it is not possible to make use of the routines elaborated to inspect manipulations of paper documents in the IT-environment.

The information within a paper document is normally directly transcribed from *a human thought process*, while computer materials often are the result of automatic processing that at times may not be directly connected to human thought. It could on occasion be difficult to obtain information about how the user intended to process stored text-data and computer programs. When material in readable form is used as evidence the adverse could raise objections to the use of certain keywords etc. If no material exists about how the system is intended to be used, the flexibility of computer programs probably will make it hard to prove that a certain constellation of information was intended.

2.3.5 Concealed demands

Issues concerning "electronic documents" have, as mentioned, been made topical in connection with provisions regarding document forgery. Work with recommendation No. R (89) 9 on computer related crime[7] clarified the fact that forgery in different countries was treated in completely different ways. In some countries the concept "document" according to criminal law has been expanded by adding data, disks or some such formulation to an existing definition (e.g. England, Finland, Greece, Portugal and Switzerland). In other

---

5 The self-dependent existence of a paper document stores certain information separate from other physical objects while the relations between text, "signature" and carrier in an electronic document is not univocal and "locked" in the same way.

6 The user of a system normally has no idea about how the physical storage is arranged. In advanced databases, for example relational databases, it is possible even to make changes in the stored state without changing the readable state when the user gives the computer command to print out a document or to show it on a screen.

7 Cf. footnote 3.

countries certain provisions, or a thorough revision of the document definition, are made or suggested with bearing on IT and criminal law (e.g. Germany, France and Sweden).

An examination of legislation regarding paper documents shows that there may exist concealed demands in the traditional definitions of "document", "record", "deed", "instrument" etc. that might be difficult to apply to computer data. For example, the addition to these definitions of "the same will apply to computer data", will hardly solve the different legal issues that arise within the IT-environment, as these demands are connected with the qualifications within a written document that often are missing in an electronic document.

It is an implicit qualification within the document that it shall give *self-dependent existence* to the information and via its physical boundaries provides a clear distinction from other physical objects. One must be able to determine

- what is a single document and what are multiple documents; where are the borderlines
- what is a portion of a document instead of the entire document?

It appears however from the descriptions of the new dimensions in the IT-environment that such distinctions may be impossible to find in the stored state. Given the readable form, the contents will be structured and completed by computer programs. It is practically meaningless to search for an IT-entity which under different circumstances corresponds to a paper document, without using certain technical procedures, giving a "lock" for the data that are representing the actual document.

One additional demand that must be satisfied in order to qualify a record as a document is that it must have a certain *durability*. However, transitory text upon a screen or the swiftly fading words from a computer-generated voice will hardly fulfil these demands. While transferring certain data kept in the secondary storage of a computer to the main storage, this data is read and then deleted. A "copy" is used for the data processing. Such representation, as well as the signals representing a message during transferral via networks, is also worth legal protection.

In order to qualify a record as a document in important procedures such as the documentation of medical information, the record must also have the ability to *convince of its authenticity*; to give the reader reasons to believe that the text actually originates from the individual who, according to the record, is seen to be the issuer. A traditional document as carrier of the information is often furnished with such characteristics, i.e. a signature that indicates the authenticity of the contents.

A data file on the other hand normally has no such "lock" for the representation of the information that will render a manipulation more difficult. Manipulation of data leaves no traces, and in the computer environment one has tried to overcome the lack of controllability in two principally different ways; by general security measures and by technical methods of verification built upon encryption techniques and the bit pattern that represents the information. The fundamental idea is to create electronic signatures and other digital substitutes for the characteristics that confer confidence in a paper document.[8]

A universal solution to the legal questions concerning authenticity in the IT-environment demands a further analysis of the characteristics that confer confidence.

8 On the top of it one will find that the concept document is complicated already in the traditional paper environment.

2.3.6 Original and copy

This discussion also leads to the implicit qualification of the document concept that it shall be an *original*. The meaning of an original in an IT-environment has been discussed in various contexts. Many have not fully understood that all information is broken down to ones and zeros and that it is only a pattern of digital signals that is of interest. In other words; the unique aspect is related to a unique pattern of data — the original *content* — rather than to unique physical *examples*. Consequently, the function of a paper document to transmit authority, as a physical example — an original — can not in a simple way be recreated digitally, if the mobility will be preserved. For that reason certain applications, such as a doctor's prescription and shipping documents, demand some form of registration in the IT-environment; as the functionality within project Bolero shows.[9] Another possible method of preserving this function is in principle to substitute the functions related to the possession of a unique and tangible piece of paper by the exclusive and personal knowledge of a non-tangible secret code which is given only to the person who has the authority.

2.3.7 The character of data

The discussed document problem leads to the delineation of the term "data". According to the International Organisation for Standardisation (ISO)[10] *data* is defined as a reinterpretable representation of information in a formalised manner suitable for communication, interpretation, or processing while *information* is defined as knowledge concerning any object, such as facts, events, things, processes, or ideas including concepts, that within a certain context has a particular meaning.

The word data has, by concentrating on the representation, been given a concrete meaning, while information is seen as something abstract, i.e. knowledge.

The difficulty in understanding the nature of data depends on the fact that we are moving in the borderland between concrete and abstract objects where some of the self-evident presumptions that a traditional viewpoint is built upon, do not exist. A magnetic loading on a data carrier may be seen as something physical but hardly the non-existence of such a loading. Similar questions arise in other areas, such as electrical power distribution. The routines for data processing and the provision of electricity have in common the use of natural phenomenon where the "material" is seen partly as concrete, partly as abstract. A magnetic loading that is taken out of the technical procedure is normally seen as non-existent, while a certain magnetic loading lacks the property of physical uniqueness.

2.3.8 Differing national solutions

An overview of the laws that have been put in place, or are presently being developed, to deal with digital signatures and electronic documents in the 15 member States of the European Union shows us that only a few countries have made any progress substantial progress on the development of laws, despite the fact that the European Union and UNCITRAL have both produced draft harmonising legislation on the subject. It also shows that those laws that have been drafted address electronic documents and digital signatures generally, and not just in relation to health care.

---

9 A project sponsored within the INFOSEC-program of the CEC, dealing with electronic management of bills of lading.

10 ISO/IEC DIS 2382-1.2.

Some countries have adopted the philosophy that no new laws need to be enacted to deal with digital signatures because their existing national legal framework deals adequately with documents and signatures generally and is, moreover, flexible and broad enough to accept digital signatures and electronic documents already. But others view electronic signatures and digital signatures as completely new concepts, for which new legislation must be enacted.

Among those countries which have actually enacted legislation or who are developing draft digital signature laws at present, two basic approaches seem to have evolved:

- to only define the most important concepts such as "electronic document"; "digital signature" and "trusted third party" and set out regulations governing just their attribution, role and use;
- to define and regulate in detail the use of electronic documents, digital signatures and trusted third parties as well as to define what kinds of acts such a system could be applied to, where and when an agreement is concluded, liabilities as between the parties and so on.

It is only in Germany and Italy that the digital signature is already legally accepted for general purposes. In other countries a digital signature be used instead of the traditional hand-written signature only in specific areas. In Sweden for example, the concept "electronic document" has been defined in e.g. the Customs Act and in the provisions concerning taxation.

2.3.9 Quasi-material "data-locations" and mail-receiving functions

The quasi-material character of data raises the question of whether or not "data-locations" legally should be treated as the equivalent of traditional closed places of storage in connection with electronic delivery of messages.

In a traditional environment, a document normally is *deemed to have been received* by an agency the day upon which the document is (physically) delivered to the agency. This rule may also be applied when a diskette is mailed via the postal service to an agency.

In those cases where messages are transmitted via an electronic network, the principle applied could be that the document is deemed to have been received by the agency:

- **when it is available by the authorities technical resources such as computers and networks, or**
- **when the data, which represents the document, have reached the agency's electronic mail-receiving function.**

These rules and regulations should be applicable whether this receiving function is physically located in the agency's information system or has been relegated to a mediating company which furnishes a service in which the "mailbox" is physically located on the mediating company's premises.[11]

---

[11] As an example a Swedish governmental committee, the IT-committee, has suggested new procedural provisions which primarily correspond to current legal practice. According to this bill a document that is transmitted electronically is deemed to have arrived to an agency that day when the document (1) has arrived at the agencies *electronic address*, (2) has been received by a qualified employee, or (3)

2.3.10 Documents and electronic commerce

2.3.10.1 New patterns of commerce

The introduction of IT within the civil law area, concerning the creation of security in contract formulation, has not been limited to the conversion of traditional routines to their electronic equivalents. Instead, the entire pattern of commerce is transformed, and the focus of change becomes automatic *processes*, rather than *products* such as bids, contracts, invoices, bills of lading, etc.

The same issues arise in the health care sector when purchasing goods and services necessary for the business, and the striving to utilise the entire potential for rationalisation that IT offers has led to a balancing between efficiency and security that, in some cases, may need to be re-evaluated.

2.3.10.2 EDI-agreements

Several international organisations have attempted to solve the legal questions that arise by constructing model contracts on how contracts should be entered into, such as the so-called EDI agreements. Among other things, these contracts deal with questions that arise when involved parties enter into agreements automatically, i.e. when computers generate and transmit messages that result in a binding agreement.

Electronic commerce will most likely, at least in certain areas, attain such dimensions that it will hardly be possible to initiate and preserve written EDI agreements with every business associate. Therefore, there is a need for a functioning legal structure even within civil law concerning IT based routines.

2.3.10.3 Contract law

Not every detailed question can be answered in advance, but contract law is in most counties formulated at a general level and is limited to basic principles, which are appropriate for agreements of varying type. Questions that do not directly fit under any of the prevailing regulations may still be able to be dealt with in close relation to the principles upon which contract law is based.

Regarding the question of whether or not electronic manifestations of a party's "will", generated automatically without direct human involvement, can result in binding contracts, a parallel can be drawn with such traditional "mass" transactions that occur frequently and in large volume in daily practice. Typical contracts that fall into this group are such things as small, simple purchases in stores or a bus trip paid in cash.[12] Consider whether or not a healthcare establishment should be bound by an offer or reply that is electronically and automatically made. The purpose of the entire procedure is to create binding agreements when certain exterior circumstances combined with one another function as the direct establishment of a contract. Could law and praxis in different

---

may be assumed to have arrived at the agencies electronic address, if it has come into the hands of a qualified employee on the following working day. The concept "electronic address" is suggested as a quasi-material function — independent of the physical location.

12 It may also be cited from Swedish jurisprudence that a contract regarding parking is deemed to be entered into by simply placing the car in a parking place; see also a Swedish governmental report by the IT-committee (SOU 1996:40 p. 117-138), discussed on the 34:th Nordic Assembly of Lawyers, Stockholm, August 21-23, 1996.

countries be sufficiently accommodating to allow a non-prejudicial application of contract law, at the same time avoiding a new construction that departs from traditional civil law?[13]

2.3.11 Data and procedural law

The nature of data and its effect on the procedural code has in most countries not yet been closely discussed. When computer materials are actualised as documentary evidence or within seizure, one central question is the determination of the object of a proceeding. Is it:

- the data carrier/the computer
- the stored example of data, or
- the bit pattern, without attachment to a particular physical example that represents the stored information?

In some countries key words in procedural law (e.g. "anything corporeal") have bearing on certain physical objects, diskettes, hard discs, etc., while the terms in other procedural laws also cover quasi-material objects. The traditional starting point of the carrier of the information will at times lead to results that are undesirable and in conflict with the principle of proportionality: Shall the computer be seized or be an object of edition though only one file is of interest and probably could be copied in a secure way? A fundamental starting-point from the perspective of the data itself rather than that of the data carrier or hardware is therefore to avoid legal and practical obstacles.[14]

In addition, a unified point of view concerning the IT-objects is desirable, by preference a definition of "document" that could be universally accepted. It would most likely simplify international co-operation and aid in the creation of distinct regulations in the IT-environment.

---

13 The aforementioned Swedish IT-committee also found the following: Certain provisions in contract law lose their purpose when contracts are entered into completely automatically. These are the provisions that presuppose human behaviour patterns, such as those dealing with coercion, deceit and usury. A computer, for example, cannot threaten another computer. However, this does not necessitate any amendments in Swedish contract law since irrational results may be corrected through the so-called general clause, which is completely free from subjectivity. — Also in other areas current contract law should be applicable to the IT area. For example, this is true concerning provisions regarding liability because a transmitted message is delayed or never received, as well as provisions dealing with "written" and "oral" communication. — The committee suggests, however, an amendment in contract law concerning the question of who is liable when an electronic message has been corrupted during transmission. A complementary addition to the current provisions concerning assignment of risk due to the delay or disappearance of a message is recommended. This provision should also be applicable when a message is corrupted during transmission to the receiver (Section 40 of the Contract Law). The Contract Law will then correspond to the present Swedish Law of Contract of Sale of Goods, which came into force in 1990. The same solution in Law of Contract of Sale of Goods is adopted in the other Nordic Countries.

14 The interpretation in an IT-environment of wordings in procedural laws, elaborated prior to computerisation, often seem to focus upon diskettes and other hardware, as if computer-data is recorded and structured in the same way as a paper document. The increasing awareness of the quasi-material character of data together with a desire to avoid practical and legal obstacles in proceedings have made the need for a starting-point from the data itself more manifest. Relevant indicators may be seen in praxis: The seizure of a hard disk filled with sensitive data is normally not acceptable when only a limited portion of the data is needed.

2.4 The European Union draft Directives on digital signatures and on electronic commerce

A proposal for a Directive establishing a harmonised European legal framework for the use of electronic signatures was put forward (on 13 May 1998) by the European Commission, on the initiative of Telecommunications Commissioner Martin Bangemann and Single Market Commissioner Mario Monti. At the time of writing the national delegations of the council is negotiating the final wording of a revised proposed directive.

The proposed Directive comes as a follow up to the Communication *on Ensuring security and trust in electronic communication — Towards a European framework for digital signatures and encryption* adopted by the Commission in October 1997.[15] That Communication identified the lack of security on electronic networks as being one of the major obstacles impeding the rapid development of electronic commerce.

By laying down minimum rules concerning security and liability, the proposed Directive aims to ensure that electronic signatures are legally recognised throughout the EU on the basis of the Single Market principles of free movement of services and home country control. The proposal would therefore create a framework for secure on-line transactions throughout the Single Market and so stimulate investment in electronic commerce services with ensuing benefits for the EU in terms of growth, competitiveness and employment.

If adopted, this Directive will hopefully remove one of the main remaining obstacles to the widespread take-up of electronic commerce and provide a basis for a trustworthy health communication. The proposal is timely because most Member States, as we have documented in this report, have yet to set up a legislative framework for electronic signatures. It will therefore ensure a harmonious legal framework for the Single Market from the outset rather than having to counter potentially disparate national initiatives. However, no specific provision is made in the European Directive for the use of digital signatures and electronic documents in healthcare.

The main elements of the proposed Directive are:

2.4.1 Essential requirements

The proposal would define essential requirements for electronic signature certificates and certification services so as to ensure minimum levels of security and allow their free movement throughout the Single Market.

2.4.2 Liability

The proposal would establish minimum liability rules for service providers, who would in particular be liable for the validity of a certificate's content. This approach will ensure the free movement of certificates and certification services within the Single Market, build consumer trust and stimulate operators to develop secure systems and signatures without restrictive and inflexible regulation.

---

[15] European Commission Communication. *Ensuring security and trust in electronic communication — towards a European framework for digital signatures and encryption.* COM (97) 503 of 16 April 1997.

2.4.3 Legal recognition

The proposal would stipulate that an electronic signature could not be legally discriminated against solely on the grounds that it is in electronic form, as the legal effects of electronic signatures are essential for an open and trustworthy system for electronic signatures. If a certificate and the service provider met certain essential requirements, electronic signatures based on their service would benefit from an automatic assumption that they were legally recognised in the same manner as hand-written signatures. Furthermore they could be used as evidence in legal proceedings.

2.4.4 A technology-neutral framework

Given the pace of technological innovation, the proposal provides for legal recognition of electronic signatures irrespective of the technology used (e.g. digital signatures using asymmetric cryptography or biometrics).

2.4.5 Scope

The proposal concerns the supply of certificates to the public aimed at identifying the sender of an electronic message, but does not apply to closed user groups such as corporate Intranets or banking systems, where a trust relationship already exists and where there is therefore no obvious need for regulation.

2.4.6 Certification

Certification services could be offered in principle without prior authorisation, in view of the fact that technology and the market are evolving rapidly and as market forces will encourage high levels of security to satisfy consumers' concerns. Member States would be free to set up voluntary accreditation schemes for certification service providers in order to indicate special security measures or levels. Certification service providers wishing users of their certificates to benefit from a legal recognition of signatures based on their certificates would, however, have to fulfil certain essential requirements.

2.4.7 International dimension

In order to facilitate electronic commerce at the world level, the proposal includes mechanisms for co-operation with third countries on mutual recognition of certificates on the basis of bilateral and multilateral agreements.

2.4.8 The proposal for a directive on Electronic Commerce

The European Commission has also published a Proposal for a European Parliament and Council ***Directive*** on certain legal aspects of ***electronic commerce*** in the internal market. The underlying proposal was submitted by the Commission on 23 December 1998.

The Proposal (1999/C 30/04) seeks to ensure the proper functioning of the internal market, particularly the free movement of Information Society services between the Member States.

It approximates national provisions on Information Society services relating to the internal market arrangements, the establishment of service providers, commercial communications, ***electronic*** contracts, the liability of intermediaries, codes of conduct, out-of-court dispute settlements, court actions and cooperation between Member States.

This Proposal complements Community law applicable to Information Society services, without prejudice to the existing level of protection for public health and consumer interests.

Chapter two of the Proposal is divided into four different sections, outlining the principles for the Member States to follow:

- Establishment and information requirements;
- Commercial communications;
- ***Electronic*** contracts;
- Liability of intermediaries;

Three years after the adoption of this Proposal, the Commission is to submit to the European Parliament, the Council and the Economic and Social Committee, a report on the application of this ***Directive***, accompanied by proposals for adapting it to developments in the field of Information Society services.

2.5 Healthcare legislation pertinent to the current problem

As described above many of the issues regarding legal aspects of IT use in healthcare is not specific for this sector. However there are also in each country a number of healthcare specific laws relevant to the problem.

The following examples may be mentioned:

- Medical Records Acts
- Prescription Acts
- Regulation of healthcare professional responsibility

The main legal problems where difficulties arise with digital documents in the pan-European healthcare sector are:

Harmonisation of registration evidence

There should be available legal evidence that the people involved in a health care network are duly registered in their country as healthcare professionals of a certain type. This implies the setting up of electronic registers in the different countries and the development of common structures for public key certification controlled by national authorities.

These national professional registration bodies, possibly several for different professions and for regional registers should establish a pan-European collaboration where users of the healthcare sector can have access and sufficient trust to any of these. In a longer term perspective it is a goal to have such a network of healthcare professional registers operation in a truly global scale.

Harmonisation of the protection level

There is a need for a common language to describe the protection level which has to be implemented for different types of documents transmitted or consulted. Some documents may require a very high security level but some others may only require a much lower level of protection. In addition, different access rights must be possible to assign (to read or to write the data) according to the status of the healthcare professional: medical practitioner, nurse, administrator etc. and their relation to the specific patient care. While views on this policy may very between countries and even within a country, the effective policy negotiation (possibly by completely automatic means implies the definition of a common model of authorisation and technical protection.

Harmonisation of the rules for emergency access

This should enable access to the medical records in an emergency with or without a patients' consent. The security of the medical data must not decrease the security of the patient. There is a balance to establish between privacy protection and health protection. A patient must not be harmed or lose their chances of survival simply because a medical practitioner has not been able to have access to some key medical information registered in the record of the patient. In an emergency situation a procedure must be defined and controlled by a medical authority which has the ability to decide if there is a real need for emergency access to the medical record and to allow this access.

Encryption and confidentiality

The legislation concerning the encryption of data to protect their confidentiality is still different in the countries of the European Union, although an important harmonisation effort is actually being conducted at the national level. It has been stated that the harmonisation of this legislation appears to be a general problem with no medical specificities but the requirements for efficient confidentiality protection also across-borders is very high in the health sector.

Security measures for the receiver

With regard to security measures from the receivers of electronic messages, it should be required that the receiver takes the necessary measures to keep medical data secure, so that when medical data has been exchanged between sender and receiver the reciever also has obligations, evidenced by the issuing of an electronic receipt.

2.6 Conclusions

When information technology is replacing traditional paper based routines many legal aspects need to be reconsidered. However, a deeper analysis reveals that in fact most of the basic concepts in our existing legislations are still valid in the information society.

The basic requirement to be able to prove authenticity of a document is very high on the agenda when planning for the further use of telematics in health. This includes the preservation of data integrity and the ability to prove who issued a document. Digital signatures and public key infrastructures appear to be a good and today only realistic solution to this basic requirement.

There is still a major need for adaptations of legislation in many European states, both general and healthcare specific. However, directives on electronic signatures and electronic commerce have been proposed in 1998 by the Commission and are presently being finalised by the Council. This will most likely provide a good basis for harmonised legislation in the member states in the following years providing no 1 for the possible legal acceptance of electronic documents in all situations. In addition, detailed technical specifications in the form of international standards will need to be agreed to help interoperability and interpretation of legislative requirements by the judicial system. The Commission has issued a mandate to the European standardization bodies to develop a plan for this.

The certification service providers and end user systems for generation of digital signatures may need to be controlled by third party testing and certification, possibly under some governmental control to facilitate the acceptance by the courts. The present draft directive however emphasises the importance of market developments in the information security area.

One area where the healthcare sector must take action itself without delay is to start to develop a system with cross border recognition for legally acceptable proofs of professional registration for doctors, nurses, pharmacists etc. This will most likely require digital signature techniques and the linkage to appropriate bodies for issuing of such professional rights as they exist in the different member states.

It should also be clearly stated that there is no reason for healthcare organisations to await further evolution of regulation of digital documents. In order to meet the basic requirements of existing legislation, prepared for centuries of experience with paper routines the rapid introduction of digital signature techniques is advisory.

3. Trends in Health Telematics

Torleif Olhede and Gunnar O. Klein

3.1 Introduction to health networks

3.1.1 Basis for the analysis

This chapter is based on the studies made during the HealthPlans concerted action which was a part of the Telematics Applications Programme of the European Commission with some material from the RHINE (Regional Health Information Networks for Europe) project funded by DGIII. The role of the HealthPlans concerted action was to assist user groups (healthcare authorities, the industrial sector and end-user organisations) who are participating in the pilot and implementation activities funded by the European Commission, in most cases also supported by national and regional R&D funds. These key actors found in the concerted action a forum where a consensus could be reached on principles and requirements, where a common methodology could be developed to monitor progress and validate the results of the pilot projects, and where information, experiences and plans for the establishment of healthcare telematics systems and services could be shared.

3.1.2 Definitions of Networks

The word "Network" is often used with different meanings:

a) Physical link and basic communication protocol services: (The infrastructure of copper or optical fibre, often provided by a general service provider, initially only telephone companies but now more and more also by other organisations, e.g. cable TV operators.
b) content providers (example: knowledge data bases in healthcare).
c) group of individuals or organisations interested in communicating with each other in a specific domain

In addition some countries use the concept of "care network" that does not imply necessarily a telecommunication network but means a formal or informal association between different healthcare actors like hospitals, out-patient clinics and GPs, community nursing etc. to offer a complete set of complementing services.

3.1.3 Cards and networks

3.1.3.1 Complementary — not alternatives

Machine readable cards have sometimes been regarded as an alternative network but they should rather be considered as an important complement to the traditional data networks.

Globally, there is a major interest in using particularly smart card technology for large programs in Healthcare because of its security features.

There are two application domains:

1 the Patient Data Card (PDC),
2 the Health Professional Card (HPC).

These are to be thought as two distinct cards with different specifications but they also can be looked at as applications that may exist in a physical card that can handle more than one application.

3.1.3.2 Patient data cards

The major large scale uses of patient data cards in e.g. Germany, France and Spain have been to ensure a secure proof of entitlement to care through various types of insurance systems. In this aspect the patient data cards are used to support an electronic claims processing over traditional networks. In addition some projects have also stored some medical data on the card itself e.g. for emergency purposes. However one of the recent trends which can be seen in different countries is:

- less data in the patient cards, as far as no medical data,
- more pointers to other healthcare providers with telephone numbers or network addresses to data bases, directories or other services where additional information can be found.

Nevertheless, the large programs are currently being implemented in using both data and pointers on the card.

It is likely that patient held cards will also be used more in the future as security devices e.g from the home PC to different telematic services. These may be similar to healthcare professional cards but may also be general purpose electronic ID cards used e.g. for home banking or Electronic Commerce.

3.1.3.3 Health Professional Cards

In recent years there has been a lot of interest in many European countries in the so called health professional cards. The core functions of such cards used to provide secure use of networks are:

- identification and authentication of the card holder,
- electronic signature,
- confidentiality mechanisms provision.

In addition health professional cards may in some countries be used to provide an off-line proof of professional status e.g. as a registered physician.

Implementation of Health professional cards in a country implies the development and provision of Trusted Third Party services. International cross border recognition of Health professional cards requires also mutual recognition of National Trusted Third Parties. The holders of the directory services may, for reasons of efficiency, also be the Trusted Third Party function holders.

3.2 Benefit areas of Health Telematics for the national and regional health authorities

3.2.1 Healthcare reorganisation

National and regional healthcare authorities are looking for telematics solutions to the problems raised by healthcare reorganisation and by the increased expectations from the general public for an improved quality of healthcare services.

Information Technologies (IT) enable the provision of meaningful accurate information for:

- Epidemiological surveillance and health monitoring;
- Health promotion and disease prevention;
- Environmental health;
- Early detection, diagnostics, care and cure of individual patients;
- Analysis of health policy, and
- Health administration and management.

3.2.2 Stepwise Development

Healthcare organisations are under constant budgetary pressure. Generally, available budgets are inadequate to pay the high one-time capital costs of complete new information systems. Therefore regional authorities prefer to develop information systems stepwise, incrementally integrating additional applications in accordance with expressed needs and budgetary possibilities. Such a strategy would enable Regions to choose the best of breed software from different 'European' suppliers, and to optimise in this way the price performance ratio and quality of their information systems.

3.2.3 Responsiveness to Change

The health sector in most, if not all, European countries is in transition. These changes refer to all areas of the health systems: delivery of healthcare, organisation, development and allocation of resources, economic support and financing, as well as administration and management. Such developments are putting therefore a high demand on the functionality, interrelationships and architectures of regional information systems and their responsiveness to change.

3.2.4 Health monitoring and management of quality and cost

From the viewpoint of health management, regional information systems should enable monitoring (and surveillance) of health and disease, and support 'geographical epidemiological' analyses of the differences in the incidence and prevalence of disease between and within Regions in all relevant areas. The health situation, quality of care, and costs can only be measured if the desired levels can be defined against which achievements can be compared. Regional information systems should therefore provide for such analyses, identifying reasons for variation. Knowledge-based and decision support systems should be part of regional information systems as well.

3.2.5 Active patients as telematics users

Empowerment of patients to take an active role in their own healthcare is recognised as of growing importance by patients as well as by professionals. Provision of appropriate information at the right times can ensure that patients are aware of the potential benefits and risks associated with options for their future care. Patients increasingly (and rightly) expect more from the health service. They want to be informed what is available, what they can expect and when they can expect it. Patient legislation in some European countries defines patients' rights in this respect and set out rules which aim to ensure that patients receive timely and appropriate care. This creates further demands for accurate and timely health information. Appropriate IT to meet these expectations is hardly available but in many regions world wide web based services to the general public are currently being developed.

3.2.6 Past and future trends in Europe

The major IT policies and integration strategies and technologies for healthcare information systems since 1970 can be summarised as follows:

1970-1980: National solutions initiated and supported by government IT policies and strategies, initially restricted to patient administration systems, billing and payments in hospitals;

1980-2000: Free choice, resulting in 'fragmentation', which characterises the European health IT market, both in demand and supply;

Beyond 2000: Free choice, based on common (European) reference architectures, European and international standards including security techniques and management guidelines.

3.3 Concerns in implementing regional health telematics

3.3.1 Major problem areas

The higher the quality of information that can be achieved, the better is the health and care that can be expected. In spite of the great potential of IT in healthcare, health IT is characterised by its failures rather than by its successes. Problems are of two kinds, namely those of the market in general, and those specific of the Regions. The general problems arise in six main areas:

- Collection of data and use of information;
- Quality of information systems;
- Growing public expectations;
- Security and confidentiality;
- Lack of standards;
- Procurement and implementation of systems.

3.3.2 Region-specific concerns

- Different requirements of the differing components of regional information systems and networks;
- Region-wide coverage and interoperability;
- Co-operation between differing types of organisations (public and private)
- Access by authorised users only, independent of their position within the regional healthcare organisation;

3.3.2.1 Specific Needs of Different Units

As a Region is typically a distributed entity, its health IT system will also be distributed, creating information for users on different levels and in various geographical locations, using data spread all over the Region. The system will involve software running on different computers installed in different physical locations. Modularity and interoperability of these different modules are therefore major requirements.

3.3.2.2 Region-wide Coverage and Interoperability

As health is the combined result of the health sector itself and other health-related sectors (e.g. environmental agencies), data needs to be exchanged between these entities. Such data exchange is taking place at the same horizontal level. However, there is also an exchange of data in a vertical direction between various administrative levels, both 'above' Regions with National Administrations as well as 'within' Regions with the Local Administrations, including City governing bodies and statistical offices.

Data exchange in healthcare is usually not so easy, as experience demonstrates in Regions where networks to link data already exist. Generally, systems are fragmented and existing data networks are based on a range of different technologies and standards. To make matters worse, the networks in different Regions are usually not interconnected so that they cannot support national (or local) applications without being upgraded or extended, with substantial additional cost. Regional information systems receive data input from health professionals, environmental agencies, health and social services institutions and from financial bodies, both public and private. In return, they provide their data to these persons and organisations.

Finally, Regions serve their citizens. Therefore good communication between the all components of a regional information system must be seen as a paramount requirement. Regional information systems should therefore offer Region-wide coverage and provide interconnectivity between the data bases concerned, i.e. interoperability.

If this funtioned satisfatorily then Regions could protect their investments in existing products (legacy systems) and avoid replacement. Good communication between the components of a regional information system must be seen as paramount. It is essential that regional information systems offer Region-wide coverage and provide interconnectivity between the data bases concerned, i.e. interoperability. Purchasing an integrated system from a single supplier is one way of achieving this. Interconnecting individual applications from different vendors is the other. There are pros and cons to each. In practice, fully integrated single systems have proved unsuitable in most Regions because of their high costs and long lead times. Regions should therefore seek to avoid replacing existing products (legacy systems) in order to protect their investments, provided these existing systems can be made to work satisfactorily within the regional context.

Hence, regional information systems should be built on the basis of common 'integration' platforms, independent of machines and vendors, enabling interconnection with already existing solutions using different technologies. Such an open information infrastructure should not only include networking aspects but also the basic 'common' software layers, and apply European standards.

3.3.3 National Solutions: Past

At the start of large-scale application of IT in healthcare, i.e. in the early 70's, governments in European countries tried to control development by the nation-wide introduction of a common patient administration system. This was introduced in order to register and identify patients, and to facilitate billing and paying (or reimbursement). The required software was ordered centrally and provided by a single vendor for national use, or regional computer centres were introduced to serve large groups of connected hospitals on the basis of shared, proprietary central mainframe computers. However, connectivity to the national systems has proven to be rather difficult, and due to the progress of IT, the systems became rapidly out of date. Therefore these national solutions tended to inhibit and constrain development rather than promote it. Moreover, this strategy raised resistance amongst users as well as providers. The result was that this policy was abandoned in all Western countries.

3.4 Success factors for the future

3.4.1 Free Choice based on Common Reference Architectures and Standards

The disadvantages of fragmentation and small scale have first been recognised by the Commission of the European Union, and more recently also by national governments, notably: by the governments of the Nordic countries, UK and France, as well as by the governments of the Central and Eastern European countries. In the Nordic countries and the UK national policies are currently directed at the establishment of national and even international telematics service networks to connect healthcare provider organisations, payment organisations and administrations for 'open' voice mobile and data communications. At institutional level the development towards 'open' information systems on common architectures and national implementation guidelines of European standards is promoted to facilitate the introduction of electronic patient records e.g in Sweden.

3.4.2 Focus on the needs of the end-users

For end-users, including citizens, patients and healthcare professionals, it is important to identify those factors that are critical to the acceptance of the developed systems. Social, legal, cultural, professional and ethical issues must be taken into account to remove possible obstacles and to ensure a widespread perception of the benefits of healthcare telematics for all those involved. A continuous and continuing programme to educate professionals and citizens to the benefits of healthcare telematics and how these can be achieved are key elements in reaching these objectives.

3.4.3 Building consensus

A consensus making process starts with a group of experts and representatives of different institutions public or private and they represent both their own point of view and the point of view of their institution and their country. The process is never complete and should continue after the workshop has finished and the report is published. If it is re-done in say two years, it may well come to different conclusions and recommendations.

3.4.4 Making use of inter-sector developments

The development of specific healthcare telematic services should rely on a common telematic infrastructure for generic applications already being available regionally or nationally through the Telecom operators. The supporting actions should concentrate on value added services and applications, by developing and validating dedicated services that could be plugged onto the existing infrastructure.

In some countries or regions, "special" healthcare networks are being built to reflect the physical links. However, in many cases this has not really meant that specific major trunk cablings are made but techniques such as Virtual Private Networks (VPN) create logical networks for healthcare parties.

An important issue under discussion in many countries is whether the public Internet can be used for routine healthcare telematics. Because of the lack of readily available security services there has generally been a great concern and at the policy level a reluctance to use Internet.

The modern cryptographic security services described in this booklet may provide sufficient protection in order for this very affordable resource to be used also in healthcare. It may however also be demonstrated that the traffic and value-added services generated by the healthcare sector will warrant some specific tailoring of generic services. Some examples are dedicated security systems for authorisation and access control, and to provide sufficient means of assuring availability of the required bandwidth e.g. for realtime video-conferencing or for bridging cabled and wireless networks to the internal networks of healthcare establishments.

3.4.5 Ensuring Security and Confidentiality

Personal health information is highly sensitive. Without proper control, and legislation, information stored in computerised information management systems is more readily accessible to outsiders than the same information stored in manual filing systems, and linkages between computerised records for the same person can be more easily established. This development has increased public and professional concerns with regard to security and confidentiality. It is of particular importance to protect information that is exchanged in open information systems and networks.

3.4.6 Using standards to ensure interoperability

The significant gains that are possible from healthcare information systems will only come about if systems are able to reflect real business processes and are integrated. This will mean adoption of and adherence to certain agreed standards. There are two groups of standards that matter: technical standards and semantic standards.

Technical standards allow dissimilar computers to communicate. There is no shortage of standards to adopt. However, generally healthcare institutions have been slow to adopt policy on common standards. Moreover, present systems on offer are largely proprietary systems developed without application of national or international standards. This makes it difficult to link systems and machines. In practice, many developers have created devices for linking technically unlike systems, and so the problem has been solved piecemeal and only at a tactical level. But, as the number of different systems grows, the cost of linking them in this way will become prohibitive, unless common standards have been adopted by both users and suppliers which can support strategic integration.

Security includes the three levels: services, functions and mechanisms. Handshaking protocols including policy bridging, cryptographic functions also including smart cards, certification service provisions and directory services.

Exchange formats Standards for healthcare message content and syntax are extremely important and a lot is already available or in the pipeline to be finalised very soon. The new suite of standards for Electronic Healthcare Record Communication will also be very important. Archiving formats may also facilitate communication.

Domains where standards are to be recommended in the long term but perhaps not to be made compulsory are the Architecture of Health Information Systems (HISA) and various frameworks for development. The general purpose middleware solutions from OMG (Corba) or Microsoft (COM/DCOM) will also be important facilitators of communication.

Semantic standards relate to the meaningful exchange of data from different sources. This creates problems that are much less easy to solve, in particular if healthcare institutions have developed their own coding systems or (as most of them do) have 'passively accepted' any coding system that may have been incorporated in the application software they have purchased.

Terminology and concepts classification and coding systems, e.g. for diagnosis, medicinal products and prescriptions, medical procedures and more generally all nomenclatures including medical equipment to be used at the national and international level. What is needed is a harmonised European approach.

3.5 Conclusions

Networks for health telematics is a key feature of the strategy for health systems of the next millenium and will provide enabling capabilities in a range of benefit areas. There are some concerns particularly at regional levels about how telematics can be implemented ensuring interoperability of all actors, and security is one major part of this concern. The way ahead has to be about choice and flexibility within a framework of using standards. Different system solutions, reflecting different technical generations and suppliers must be able to coexist and communicate. However, certain secure technology services and a public key infrastructure does require firm and convergent planning to enable this. Only then can information delivery be ensured which can be tailored to be useful across different needs from collaborating healthcare professionals to citizens/patients and to the planners/ politicians.

Case Studies of Security Problems and their Solutions
G.O. Klein (Ed.)
IOS Press, 2000

4. The CoCo Guide to EDI Security

Tor Olav Grotan

4.1 Abstract

This chapter describes the approach and contents of the regional EDI security guidelines developed in the CoCo project. The chapter also presents some Norwegian experiences in view of the guidelines making use also of the TrustHealth 1 recommendations.

The security guide provides a framework for regional projects, with a main objective to indicate how and to which extent, existing and standardised (EDI message) security techniques, security infrastructure (in terms of Trusted Third Parties), Codes of Connections, common Security Polices and Codes of Conduct for the individual, collectively can facilitate the pursuing of the principles of the (1995) EU Directive on the protection of individuals, in health care telematics projects.

4.2 Introduction

The guideline was intended to allow regional projects to adopt the components appropriate to meeting local objectives, whilst ensuring no work is duplicated to meet the strategic objectives of CoCo.

It was believed that as health care professionals are relatively mobile, the smartcard format facilitates the need for key and certificate distribution, as well as other information associated with the healthcare professional.

The intended audience was telematics service providers and the managers in charge of the local healthcare telematics networks and infrastructural services, as well as the providers of user-oriented services.

Documents produces by the TrustHealth1 [4] project has been one of the major sources and references for the work.

4.3 Security perspective

4.3.1 The rationale for security in healthcare telematics networks

Both users, suppliers and governments highlights the fundamental role of information management and technology in transforming the management and delivery of health care. Apparently, the immediate challenge is to harness the potential benefits of interconnection.

The security issue is however a crucial part of this challenge. The paramount importance of securing the *trustworthiness of the information flow*, in terms of credibility, accountability, quality, integrity, liability and authenticity, is quite obvious, while preserving confidentiality, privacy and patient integrity.

The delivery of health services however requires that information is able to circulate relatively freely and effectively between *authorised* users, and a patient's life may depend on the rapid delivery of information. A telematic system has a unique capability to facilitate such an information flow.

The security challenges are immediate in the sense that they have to be addressed from the very beginning of a healthcare telematics project. The security issue is also a long term issue requiring continuous attention, and always calling for a long-term perspective and a proper balance between the different (legitimate) needs and the technology potential.

4.3.2 Security objectives and challenges

The use of telematics in health care will modify the existing pattern of relationships between healthcare professionals and their patients.

The traditional professional secrecy — based on a confidential patient-doctor relationship — is no longer a sufficient platform, and the lack of a legal framework to adequately regulate the new situation is a substantial problem.

A healthcare telematics project should therefore constitute and operate an organisational security management framework[16]. Such a framework should — in a concerted manner — combine technical, administrational, legal and ethical security aspects, despite the fact that the establishment of legal requirements in this field is in its very beginning.

4.4 Legal and Liability issues[17]

The legal challenge is to establish frameworks and regulations with instrumental capacities in organising the relationships between all the different actors, taking into account their legitimate needs and the risks created by the different usage of telematic networks and services. Obviously, there will be conflicting needs and demands, as well as unforeseen problems.

The European Directive on the protection of personal data, enacted on the 24th of July 1995 [1] provides guidelines to all the member states, to be enacted within their national privacy regulations. The Directive clearly states that personal data has to be obtained and processed fairly, and that they might be stored for specific and legitimate purposes, but not used in a way incompatible with those purposes.

Following the Directive, some important questions are to be raised concerning professional secrecy in the electronic healthcare network:

The patient's generally admitted right to information about himself may in some situations be legally restricted, e.g. when knowledge may have a detrimental effect on his mental or physical health.

In certain cases, the divulgence of medical secrecies are authorised by law. Who shall be responsible for this in a networked environment?

The lack of legislation and authoritative recommendations, properly adapted to the IT world, may bring obstacles to the application of powerful technology, e.g. digital signatures and cryptography.

---

16 Note that a security framework of this type, in general is fundamental for the establishment and maintenance of security in a networked environment.

17 This section is widely based on [2].

Though there is a clear and pronounced need for legally accepted methods and practices for the application of digital signatures, it is likely that we will have to tolerate insufficient legislation, for a prolonged period of time. The need for new legislation to balance the *legitimate protection needs* with the need for *communications interception* in relation to national security or prevention of criminality, has been under discussion for quite a while, both nationally and on the EU level. Such regulations will have a significant impact on the development of European, national and regional health care networks.

There is also a clear need for some common regulations concerning the ownership of the medical data. E.g. when a patient data card is used for accessing the network, is the holder of the card also the owner of the information on the card?

Health care networks will heavily modify the flow of information within the healthcare system, and thus provoke the need for a redefinition of the roles and fields of practice between the professionals. The registration of professionals and the means of ensuring adequate proofs of professional status within the network must be managed by a competent authority.

4.5 The EU Directive on Data Protection[18]

4.5.1 Background

The Security Guide investigated the implications of The European Union Directive 95/46/EC on the protection of individuals with regard to the processing of personal data and on the free movement of such data [1].

The Directive recognises that the use of telematics in relation to personal data in general, and especially in relation to special categories of processing as for example the healthcare sector, demands new principles, regulations and legal frameworks in order to protect personal information.

It is clear that the EU Directive will have many implications on how and to which degree medical data can be shared in healthcare networks. In order to remove the *obstacles to the free flow of personal data* on data protection grounds *caused by the divergence* between the national legislation, the Directive aims at *co-ordinating the legislation* of the different Member States to ensure an equivalent level of protection.

The EU directive will in many respects serve as a common denominator for its member states and associated states/countries, and we will therefore briefly examine the implications of the Directive when applying its requirements to a health care network.

4.5.2 The Directive's applicability for health care telematics

There is no doubt that the Directive apply for health care telematics and networks. The crucial point is however that processing of personal, health-related data, and especially in a networked context, is not characterised by standalone or atomic operations which can be uniformly measured against the requirements of the Directives. Patient information is — especially in a networked context — accessed and used in terms of sequences of operations. These sequences involve different actors from time to time, and reflect the delivery of several types of health care services, individually as well as the interactions between those

18 This chapter is widely based on [3].

services. Hence, *each of these operations must apply to the principles* laid down by the Directive *on their own terms*, with respect to legitimate purpose, conformity of data, etc.

Article 2d of the Directive states that "The Controller is the natural or legal person, public authority, agency or any other body which alone or jointly with others determines the purposes and the means of the processing of medical data". The Controller's identity is important because he is responsible for fulfilling the obligations laid down in the Directive and ensuring that the data subjects' (in our case, the patients') rights are respected. The determination of the controller also determines the national law applicable to a healthcare telematics activity or project.

When processing is carried out in the context of activities of an establishment of the Controller on the territory of a Member State, the Directive states that each state shall apply national provisions pursuant to the Directive. Where the same Controller is established on the territory of several Member States, he will have to ensure that each of the establishments respect the national law of each of these states. A Controller not established on the territory of the European Community, will have to respect the Member State's national law if he makes use[19], for the purpose of processing of medical data, of equipment situated on the territory of that Member State. Hence, the Directive seeks to avoid that a Controller circumvents the application of national law by locating himself outside the Community territory, especially when the information flow crosses national borders.

An important cornerstone of the protection afforded for the data subject is the *legitimate purpose principle*; The data must be collected for legitimate purposes and not further processed in a way incompatible with those purposes.

Article 8 of the Directive states the concerns for special categories of processing, in which health care and medical data are explicitly included. The general principle is that Member States shall *prohibit* the processing of such data, however with some exemptions. Thus, healthcare telematics projects must find grounds in article 8, enabling them to process the sensitive, medical or health care data.

Hence, it is possible to conclude that the Directive *does not prohibit* the development of healthcare telematics services involving medical, sensitive data, as long as these are sufficiently grounded in the legal systems and healthcare practices of the Member States. Still, there are many complex issues to be resolved, and the road to the answers and solutions is paved with both legal and ethical challenges.

This means that the Directive demands that a proper *balance* must be found between the legitimate right of the data subject to control the processing by means of his consent, and the need of the healthcare system to deliver its services in an effective and efficient manner, without the burden of obtaining too many explicit consents. It could for example be argued that the patient's consent is implicit by the mere fact that he is seeking a healthcare professional for help, but it may also be argued that this type of consent cannot justify that his medical data is used for insurance claims or employment purposes (other cases may be a lot more controversial!).

The Directive also lay down some principles concerning *data quality*. That is, personal data must be "*processed fairly and lawfully*", they must also be "*collected for specified, explicit and legitimate purposes*", and they must be "*adequate, relevant and not excessive in relation to valid purposes*". These aspects are highly also relevant for the construction of the EDI message flow.

Data must be "*accurate and where necessary kept up to date*". Some aspects of medical information, e.g. a GPs subjective appreciation, is difficult or even impossible to

---

19 Except for transit purposes.

qualify as "accurate". Other aspects, such as standardised nomenclature, codes, classifications and data sets to be used in medical records will depend on accurate standards, agreements and uniform practice.

Also other aspects of the Directive, such as the data subject's rights, the controller's obligations and the encouragement of codes of conduct, are highly relevant for the construction and operation of a telematics network.

4.6 Conclusions on the Directive

The conclusion of the security guide is that the Directive's scope of protection clearly goes beyond the protection afforded by traditional, professional secrecy regulations. However, the Directive does not aim to prohibit the exchange of medical data among a broad range of healthcare professionals and associates by the use of healthcare telematics, as long the telematic providers, the users and their organisations adheres the principles of the Directive. It is apparent that these principles are neither trivial nor impossible to respect and facilitate, and that the proper implementation of these principles will demand properly balanced legal and ethical frameworks and guidelines, which are not present in the current situation.

The Directive implies a greater responsibility for many actors involved in a health telematics project, as these may be considered as "controllers" and therefore liable in relation to the Directive, e.g. in order to provide for a number of data subject's rights, as well as other obligations.

However, in interpreting the Directive it should not be ignored nor forgotten that telematic systems carry the potential to be substantially more secure than paper-based systems. In our view, the challenge of a Controller is to maintain a balanced approach in order not to jeopardise the development of systems through abusive security requirements. The delivery of health services requires that information is able to circulate freely and effectively between authorised users. A patient's life may depend on the rapid delivery of information, and the Directive does not — from our judgements — aim to prohibit such benefits from the technology.

4.7 EDI security

Generally, EDI security will comprise a combination of administrative, managerial, organisational and technical measures. This security guide focus on the following aspects of EDI security:

The safe and secure utilisation of open, intermediary networks

An organisation should be able to communicate freely and securely with a selected group of other organisations and actors connected to the same open, commercial network, *without the risk of intrusion* or any other unwanted interference and intervention from other[20] actors, utilising the same (open, commercial) network.

Message security concepts applied on EDI messages

---

[20] Not belonging to the intended ("closed") community of healthcare users.

The message security *services* are exercised directly by the communicating parties in order to enforce confidentiality, integrity, identification and authentication[21] (of content or origination), accountability, access control, and non-repudiation of origin and receipt. They can be facilitated by a number of mechanisms and techniques, e.g. various encryption schemes based on symmetric or asymmetric encryption (the combination is sometimes called *hybrid encryption*. At the time of writing the security guide, EDIFACT standards were emerging, which of course were expected to be relevant for those who use the EDIFACT messages.

However, many factors argue in favour of decoupling the message security techniques, and the message internal format and syntax. Today, there is a broad consensus on the need for generic message security standards. An ongoing standardisation work in this arena is the work of prohject team 39 of CEN/TC 251 developing a European prestandard entitled *Security for Healthcare Communication*.

Controlling and conducting the purpose and legitimacy of the information (message) flow

Finally, EDI security deals with the legitimate dissemination and flow of information within the community of interconnected healthcare organisations and users. Hence, a principal goal is the *secure use of the messaging capabilities and services*. Compliance with the principles of the EU Directive with respect to e.g. the purpose of processing, is a key aspect of this.

This issue cannot be solved solely by means of (technical) access controls. Hence, the various actors must be associated by authorisations and accounting mechanisms that *frames their legitimate needs* for exchange of messages, but without abusing their professional needs. The individual user must also be provided with the means to safeguard documents he has received and are in possession of, according to the relevant principles.

4.8 Security Infrastructure

The need for infrastructural and value adding services introduces the need for *Trusted Third Parties and services* in the communication scenario. The most common focus on such services is founded on the request for *message security*, as defined in the previous chapter.

A common security infrastructure, materialising in terms of Trusted Third Party (TTP) services, facilitates the healthcare sector's secure use of common, open networks and standards. It will first of all support the implementation of EDI message security. But it will also facilitate end system and application security techniques, e.g. strong authentication and professional authorisations[22]. It may also facilitate a closer coordination between communicating organisations in terms of security policies.

On this issue, the security guide used the deliverables from the TrustHealth1 project [4] extensively. That is, we focused on:

The *basic infrastructural services* that enables and facilitates open EDI between a large number of users affiliated to various enterprises, regions or even countries. The handling of unique names, keys, certificates and cards are typical examples of services

---

21 Note that the authentication services may also be applied in other circumstances, such as for the authentication of the end user towards his or her workstation.

22 E.g., a certified GP authorisation (that is, the explicit right to prescribe strong drugs) may be needed for a pharmacy to accept an electronic prescription in terms of an EDI message, from a GP office

which are superfluous in a world where only a few parties — previously known to each other — are able to communicate. However, for large scale open EDI communication to be enabled, the infrastructural security services will be a prerequisite to establish trustworthy health telematics in a large pan-European context. At some points, we will need Trusted Third Parties (TTP) to provide some of these services.

The value adding services that are necessary to enhance the value of the actual message exchange, in order to pursue formal or legal requirements, or to avoid or resolve potential disputes between the communicating parties, associated with the message content or the interpretation of this content. The value added services can support purely (healthcare) business related conventions or agreements, or they can enact regulations given by law or by provisions of the law. Examples of such services, relevant to health care, are registration of health care professionals, issuing of professional certificates, secure storage of documents, document time stamping, claim of origin, pseudonymisation and others.

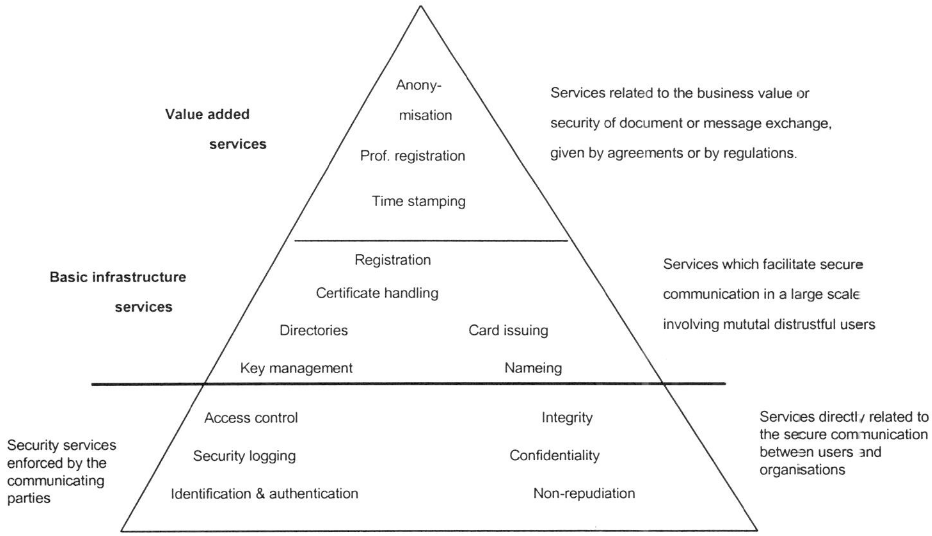

The Security Guide also outlines how the TTP infrastructure can facilitate an active (electronic) co-ordination of Security Policies between communicating parties (denoted Security Policy *Bridging* and *Negotiation*). This will contribute to the proper conduct of the information flow, and thus contribute to an even higher degree of compliance with the principles of the EU Directive.

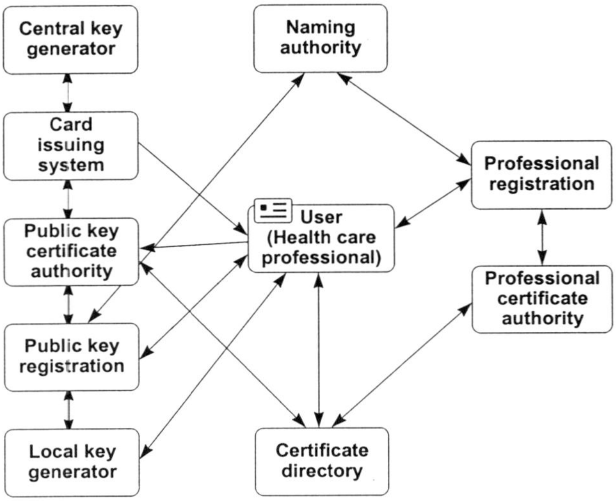

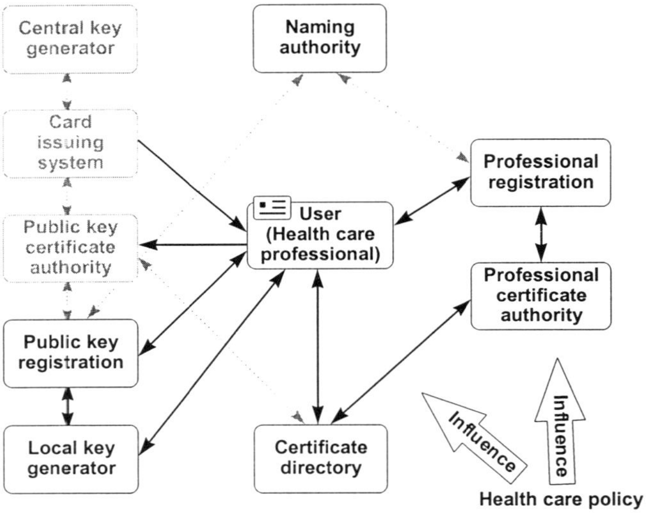

4.9 Conclusions from the security guide

This security guide concluded that the use of Codes of Connection and coordinated security policies facilitates and enables the construction of regional, logical healthcare networks and healthcare telematics user communities, based on the utilisation of open, commercial networking services.

Message security based on digital signature and asymmetric (hybrid) encryption techniques will facilitate a purpose-oriented and accountable exchange of EDI messages, which is a major requisite for the trustworthiness of the healthcare telematics in relation to the EU Directive.

The message security services require a security infrastructure. It is possible to build a purpose-oriented, distributed structure of Trusted Third Parties (TTP), in which the health care sector takes care of and emphasises its own specific needs and issues, possibly in collaboration with a more general TTP infrastructure. The infrastructure is not limited to key generation and management. Professional certification and authorisation can be supported within the same framework. The healthcare authorities can enact their responsibilities and roles trough this infrastructure, according to important principles of the EU directive.

The potential of the security infrastructure is not limited to the message security issue (in its strictest sense). It can also be used to a more differentiated, purpose-oriented and precise interaction between different (individual) users and organisations, and will provide for an even stronger compliance to the intentions and principles of the EU Directive.

Anonymisation and pseudonymisation and other value-added service further minimises the risk of EDI message exchange, and facilitates the secondary use of patient information without violating the principles of the EU Directive.

Healthcare telematics projects must be organised and managed in a way that contributes to the establishment of legal frameworks and ethical standards, Codes of Conduct that ensures a uniform practice with regard to the use of EDI message exchange and other security measures applied, is a powerful tool that facilitates the involvement of and drawing on the experiences of the medical professions.

The security of healthcare telematics project should be planned and managed as a whole. The security measures can however be introduced step by step. Codes of Connection, Network Security Policies and message security concepts, incorporating the necessary security infrastructure, are the main building bricks. A recommended approach is to start with the existing infrastructure, and develop it.

All the actors involved in the exchange of electronic medical data, individually as well as their host organisations, must commit themselves to comply with the legal requirements provided for in the European Directive on the "protection of individuals with regard to the processing of personal data and on the free movement of such data".

Trust and confidence in the concepts and actors must be established by means of a combination of initial (technical and organisational) assurances and periodical security revisions. This implies that quality assurance principles should be more emphasised than external security evaluations.

References

[1] Council of the European Union - Directive on the protection of individuals with regard to the processing of personal data and the free movement of such data. 24th July 1995.

[2] TrustHealth1 project: (Deliverable D6.1) Overview of legal issues. (Yves Poullet, Centre de Recherches Informatique et Droit (C.R.I.D.), University of Namur.)

[3] TrustHealth1 project: (Deliverable D6.2) Data Protection in Health Telematics Projects — Compliance with the European Directive on the Protection of Medical Data. (Sophie Louveaux and Yves Poullet, Centre de Recherches Informatique et Droit (C.R.I.D.), University of Namur.)

[4] TrustHealth1 project: (Deliverable D4.1) Functional Specification of TTP Services. Version 1.0.

[5] TrustHealth1 project: (Deliverable D4.2) Interface Specification of TTP Services. Version FA 4.

[6] National Health Service Executive : Code of Connection for NHS organisations, IMG E5222.

[7] The Dutch Registratiekamer: Privacy-enhancing technologies: The path to anonymity. Volume II. Rijswijk, 1995.

[8] International Journal of Biomedical Computing 43 (1996), pp 83-91: Sociotechnical aspects of the use of health related personal information for management and research. Kenneth R. Iversen and Tor

Olav Grøtan, Norwegian Centre for Medical Informatics (KITH).
[9] Norwegian Centre for EDI and Trade Procedures (Norsk EDIPRO) — Message security, digital signatures and Trusted Third Parties (in Norwegian). Kenneth R. Iversen (KITH) et al.

For more information on security of the CoCo project please contact:
Tor-Olav Grotan
E-mail: tor.o.grotan@kith.no.

5. Security Architecture of the Star Project

Paul Cooper

5.1 Abstract

This chapter provides an introduction to the Star project with a description of the project's objectives and an explanation of the continuity link through to the Intercare project. It then outlines the security service architecture developed in the Star project along with some conclusions about the common services which have been identified as needed for a regional healthcare network project.

5.2 Introduction to the Star project

The ***star*** (*Seamless Telematics Across Regions*) project's mission statement is:

> The integration, development & validation of open common telematic systems & services that enable a continuum of care for patients.

This overall goal breaks down into four main objectives:

- To understand and deliver through demonstrations, the benefits of seamless care to patients and providers.
- Integrate and develop close to market telematic service products.
- Produce generic open system solutions for heterogeneous legacy systems.
- Produce, publish and promote protocols & guidelines for interoperability.

The objectives will be achieved through the merger and application of previous EU projects and thus forms a validation of previous R&D work.

The generic telematic services represent the set of common functionalities and the associated services to be provided by the underlying information system enabling the Star project to fulfil its objectives of supporting seamless care in a telematics environment, in the following four areas:

Shared electronic patient dossier and cooperative working
Telemedicine services
Administrative services.

This is being achieved through a number of user-led demonstrator sites called satellites.

There has been a close collaboration between the satellites and the core group and many participants are in both.

The high-level objective of all satellites has been to meet the needs of the local users who have recognised the benefits of trying to manage the total care process (also know as care pathways, or seamless care). This is often driven (although not exclusively) by regional healthcare management who are wanting to optimise the use of finite resources when patients are making ever increasing demands on the available healthcare services.

The satellite's main goal is to improve the working environment of the general practitioner and the collaboration between healthcare providers treating the same patient (seamless care) by developing value-added telematic services in a user friendly open technical environment. The services are to be integrated with current applications and infrastructure.

For the two full-term satellites (Milano & West Middlesex), this objective has largely been achieved within the scope of the healthcare domains being supported. The generic services are now also available for all other satellites to implement local solutions.

In countries where service delivery is organised using a closed catchment area principle and service system is financed by local or regional authorities, it is of interest to the healthcare service providers to deliver a high level of service to the referrers of those patients. It is therefore their objective to compete in the healthcare market and this can be facilitated by the provision of region-wide telematic services. Such services may include information services from centres of excellence to those delivering care, as well as the more administrative referral, treatment and discharge services.

Star provides the necessary cohesive elements and creates bridges between a great number of information islands in the health sector. Furthermore, Star is being a catalyst in focusing the thinking of many healthcare providers. This has led to links with national projects via the new InterCare project to ensure more than a region wide implementation.

5.3 Core objectives

5.3.1 Architecture

To specify the open Star architecture for interoperability of both the generic services and for their demonstration in the satellite environments. The architecture has been completed and specifies precisely:
- the Star system users
- the services offered by the Star system to the users and the constraints that may exist between them
- the Star system components (by their external behaviour only, following the open system approach)
- the interfaces between these system components.

5.3.2 Functional Specifications

To define the functional specifications of the core services in a formalised way. This result of this work has two components — one providing a conceptual design of the functions needed by each site involved in Star, and the second providing the functional design of core telematic services able to support such needs. The functional specifications enable the definition of a local architecture for the system as well as the identification of the applications necessary to provide local support of seamless care to the users.

5.3.3 Development of Generic Services

Generic services have been developed to provide a technological environment on top of which the Star functionality can be implemented and operated. This development activity built on the results of WP3 (Functional Specifications) and WP 4 (Architecture for interoperability). This approach enables the project to deliver a truly generic approach in terms of architecture and software components which can then be implemented and operated in a variety of sites.

The Star generic servers form together the technological basis of a co-operative working environment. The project makes an intensive use of existing or emerging technologies, including results of previous projects in the European AIM Programme in which many of the Star contributors were actively involved. These developments are built on the basis of the concepts of Act Management and Patient Reference Dossier (NUCLEUS, AIM project n° 2025). These services, after having been appropriately extended and enhanced for the specific needs of Star provide the basis for the implementation of the desired cooperative working environment delivered by WP5.1. The same goes for the booking services with respect to results obtained in the SHINE (AIM n° 2035) project and the security and confidentiality services from the SESAME project (RACE n° R2051). In this sense, Star shows how existing technology components, arising from diverse sources, can be enhanced, consolidated into a single coherent single system, and deployed and validated in representative user sites.

5.4 Star and Intercare

For Star the most important link for the future is with the InterCare project — the umbrella project incorporating Cardlink 2, Hector, Star, Synapses and TrustHealth. The Intercare project started on 1st June 1998.

The InterCare project recognises that the trend of healthcare is that it is becoming more dispersed and more specialised. The factors driving this trend are both economic (large centralised hospitals are expensive) and because of the development in medical devices that enable specialist treatment to be given away from the hospital. This trend however exacerbates a problem that has long existed within the health services, namely poor (often non-existent) communication between information systems creating an environment of disjointed care just when the patient requires it to be seamless.

Taking all of these factors into account, the InterCare project is combining the results from the most important EC funded healthcare telematics projects in the areas of the electronic patient record, security, mobile communications, patient data cards, and regional telematic services in order to deliver the necessary set of integrated technologies to solve the problems facing the providers of healthcare. The emphasis is on inter-organisational care rather than intra- organisational care in recognition of the trend previously outlined.

It is well-known that there is a major paradigm shift approximately every 15 years in the world of Information Technology. In the early 1980's we had the PC revolution. In the mid 1990's we are experiencing the Internet revolution. This is having a profound effect on the way that information is perceived, used and controlled by end-users. Gone are the days when publishing was in the hands of the few — now anyone can deliver information 'on the net'. Also the concept of information always being available at source and hence always being current, has become an accepted approach. There is no need to take a copy (e.g. by file transfer, EDIFACT message, etc.) for local reference because it is now just as easy (if not easier) to obtain it as required from the originator.

These technological changes (generally described as an Internet approach) have arrived just at the time when healthcare is demanding seamless integration of systems between (inter-)organisations.

Therefore, by combining the market-driven need to gain critical mass across the spectrum of healthcare telematics rather than within a particular field, together with an emergent set of inter-organisational technological solutions, the InterCare project was born.

The healthcare telematics programme projects that are delivering their technologies to InterCare are Cardlink 2, Hector, Star, Synapses and TrustHealth. The primary objective is to achieve a convergence of results and to demonstrate & promote the synergy between these projects in six regional demonstrator sites across Europe.

These sites in Finland, Greece, Ireland, Italy, Netherlands and Sweden have been selected as they are the key national demonstration sites in each country. As such they are already committing a significant investment to prove the benefits of healthcare telematics.

In summary the InterCare project will:

- Build on the result of five complementary projects to form a new project with the necessary critical mass to integrate the results across project lines.
- Produce integrated products that will be commercialised by the industrial members of the consortium.
- Demonstrate the results at key demonstrator sites across Europe where they form an integral part of a national strategy.
- Help to solve different aspects of the problems facing the provision of inter-organisational seamless care.
- Have six demonstrator sites that will showing how the results from different fields of medical informatics combine to form the Health Information Society.

5.5 The *Star* security service

The main objectives of the *Star* security service are:

- to identify and authenticate user when requires access to a *Star* service, eg. REM, PRM, LEM, BS, ...
- to perform authorisation request when a service wants to grant access to another service on behalf of the user.
- to protect data during transfer between *Star* services
- to protect sensitive information data, eg. archives, patient dossiers, acts, ...

These objectives can be achieved through a set of functions and components based upon the technology of security in a distributed system environment resulting from the SESAME european project.

SESAME components, which should be used by the *Star* security service, will be described in the following chapters. They comprise the Security server (SS), the Public key management server (PKMS) and the Secure association context manager (SACM) implementing standard and extended GSS-APIs.

However, at the current stage the Public key management facility (PKMF) and the Cryptographic support facility (CSF) are used only by the security components itself. As their APIs are not visible to any other core service or application, their functionalities are therefore only roughly described in this document. For further reading, please refer to the SESAME document set available under:

http://www.esat.kuleuven.ac.be/cosic/sesame.html

In addition to the functionality provided by the above SESAME components, the security in *Star* environment is enriched with the Digital signature facility (DSF), which enables the protection of sensitive information with data origin, integrity and confidentiality. The function is provided through a set of high-level and generic APIs.

In the the rest of the document, an "application" or "server" or "target" can stand for any *Star* core service or user's application and "principal" can be used for both human user (e.g. GP, patient) or application.

5.5.1 The Star Security Server

The *Star* Security Server or Key Distribution center (KDC) is part of the *Star* Regional services. It provides following:

- to identify and authenticate a principal. This action is unconditionally the first step to be done by a core service or application, which wants to perform authorisation on the principal behalf.
- to generate and distribute the principal's privilege attribute certificate (PAC) to be used in the authorisation process of an application server.
- to generate and distribute cryptographic key packages to the client and server application. These key packages are needed to protect user data exchanged between the two entities.

From the architectural point of view, the KDC is composed of the Authentication Server (AS), the Privilege Attribute Server (PAS) and the Key Distribution Server (KDS)

Following functions are supported:

- identification and authentication of user or application server and providing optionally the associated PAC. The function is performed by the AS and PAS respectively.

  The initiator (eg. core service) can invoke this function via the API of the Authentication and privilege attribute Client (APA Client).
- retrieval of the server's secret key to be used in its own authentication process, which is necessary to proceed in a delegation context environment. The function is performed by the application on the local system.
- production and distribution of cryptographic keys for application client and server's association. The function is performed by the KDS. It can be invoked through the GSS-API of SACM by a Star service acting as client to talk with another service or application acting as server.

- Administration functions to manage principal (user, application), roles and privileges in the security databases. These functions can be executed using a set of interactive commands supplied by the KDC control program.

The Public Key Management server (PKMS) or Certification Authority (CA) is attached to the Regional Services and locates in the usual case on the same plattform as the Security Server. The PKM server is responsible for generation of private-public key pairs, certification of public keys and ensure adherence to the relevant security policies.

In *Star* environment, PKMS is almost in charge of:

- generation and certification of public key pairs for security server, eg. PAS's public key pair for PAC protection, KDS's key pair for interdomain working, ...
- generation and certification of subject's key pairs, which have to be used in the protection/unprotection of information data (Digital signature Facility).

There are 2 different implementations of PKMS supplied by SESAME V4:
1. the Windows Certification Authority and
2. the Unix Certification Authority.

The PKMS (CA) relies on services supplied by the Cryptographic Support Facility (CSF) and the Public Key Management Facility (PKM) for all operations related to cryptography and public keys.

5.5.1.1 The Window Certification Authority

It involves 3 servers: the Certification Authority (CA), the Certification Authority Agent (CAA) and the Local Registration Authority (LRA).

The LRA is invoked by the LRA operator using lracp control program to:

- generate a subject's public key pair.
- generate the public key certification request message.
- store the private key encrypted in the LRA's archive file.
- supply to requester a result file containing the subject's private key and its associated public key certificate returned by the CA.

The CAA is an online server run by the CAA operator using `caocp` control program. The server is responsible for the logical links between the LRA and the CA:
- handle the certification request of LRA, store in a spooler daemon and export for the CA and
- receive the response certificates generated by the CA in the spooler for the LRA

The CA is a Windows GUI application operates as an "off-line" server being responsible for:

- download certification requests (spooled messages) from the CAA.
- generate the subject's requested Directory Certificates in conformance to the relevant security policies.
- put the response into a file for transfer to the CAA.

The certification process requires

- CA's public key pair, generated by the CA installation program, where the CA public key is stored in a file, which has to be imported by other component, e.g. CAA, ..., for the later verification of signature generated by the CA
- LRA's public key pair, which is generated and certified in the usual way as described bellow.

Readers, who are looking for details on the Windows CA, is encouraged to refer to SESAME V4 Public Key Infrastructure Guide.

5.5.1.2 The Unix Certification Authority

The Unix certification process involves both SESAME administrator (`sesadm`) and Certification Authority (`ca`) unix user and uses a shell script for generation of public key pairs `config_unix_ca` and a certification program action to achieve the task.

The processing is started with the generation of the key pair and the construction of the certification request achieved via the `config_unix_ca` shell script. `config_unix_ca` can be run by the sesadm (with the exception when running for the CA itself, the login user must be `ca`). The output of the script is a certification request file, which has to be exproted and transfered to the Unix CA `action` program by whatever means to initiate the certification process.

Login as Unix CA administrator (`ca`) to run the action program. `action` generates certificates for the requested public keys and puts them in the response file `ca_response`.

The CA response file has to be sent back to the `sesadm`, who will use the pkmcp control program to import the private key and the associated public key certificate in the subject's cache.

The main objectives of the *Star* Digital Signature Facility are:
- to ensure the data origin authentication.
- to protect information data against any unauthorised alteration of its contents (integrity protection)
- to protect data confidentiality with integrity

These objectives can be achieved through a set of Application Programing Interfaces (APIs), which base on the Internet draft IDUP-GSS-API relied on the public key technology.

The *Star* Digital Signature Service is a library of functions used by an application to perform data integrity and/or privacy protection on behalf of the principal, e.g. the Act Manager AMS signs an act (integrity protection) or the Patient Dossier Server PDS protect information of a patient dossier object on behalf of the GP. Every time, when these informations are accessed, the requestor can verify and/or decrypt the information contents and ensure the origin of the data.

From the functional point of view, the Star Digital Signature facility operates in the principal associated environment and provides the following functions for protection and unprotection services:
- to perform data origin authentication (DOA) with data integrity

- to perform data confidentiality with integrity.
- to receive and verify DOA data with data integrity.
- to receive data confidentiality with integrity.

The protection service results in an opaque protection token, which can include the encrypted (initial) data in case of data confidentiality. The protection token is then to be transfered by whatever means to the receiver(s) (along with the initial data in case of DOA data with data integrity). (Note that this transfer is not in charge of the *Star* Digital Signature Service).

The protection and unprotection work with generic data unit, i.e. a stand-alone unit of data which is "independent of protection of any other data unit and independent of any concurent contact with designated receiver(s) of the data unit"[23]. They proceed in a security environment associated to the initiator or the receiver respectively.

The 2 operations are independent, i.e. the protected data unit "can be transferred to the recipient(s) — or to an archive — perhaps to be processed (unprotected) only days or years later"and "in any order over any time span" .

In this version, the data format supported by the service is the ascii textand the protected token is in conformant to PKCS#7 protocol standard.

The protection and unprotection services require:
- The principal (initiator, receiver) must possess a public key pair and certificates.
- The principal has to be authenticated to the system and possesses an appropriated Privilege Attribute Certificate (PAC).
- The receiver must be able to have access to the public key certificate of the initiator for unprotection operation.
- The initiator must be able to have access to the public key certificate of the receiver for data confidentiality with integrity protection.

The function makes use of the Cryptographic Support Facility (CSF) and the Public Key Management Facility (PKM) for all cryptography and public key related operations.

The SESAME Secure Association Context Management (SACM) or GSS Library is in charge of managing information related to the security properties of association between initiator (client) and target application (server). All such informations are maintained in a structure called the security context, which exists on both side of the association.

Functions supported by the SACM are accessible through a set of GSS-APIs. They are summarized as follows:
- peer-to-peer and/or mutual authentication
- request of privilege attributes
- data integrity and/or privacy protection
- secure transfer and handling of security attributes to be used in the access control
- delegation of rights

The SESAME GSS-APIs may be grouped in the following subsets:
1. Credential handling managing all necessary security attributes of an authenticated subject, which are hold in a structure named credentials.

[23] see internet draft: Independent Data Unit Protection Generic Security Service Application Program Interface (IDUP-GSS-API) C. Adams, Nortel

2. Security Context handling managing all security related data needed for an association between peer in security contexts, one on the client side and the second on the server side
3. protection of application dialogue concerning all application data passed between context peers
4. Security attributes handling offers the possibility to request and to fetch security attributes.

A subset of SESAME GSS-APIs, considered to be of most interest for Star core services at the current stage, will be discussed in the rest of this section [24].

The Public Key Management (PKM) Facility is a generic component issued from the SESAME V4. It is a standard link library of function in charge of all operations related to public key pair. The PKM Facility can be accessible via a set of API.

Functions supported by the PKM Facility are summarized as bellow:

1. Environment handling all necessary internal variables and memory certificate cache.
2. Keys handling to retrieve/store key pairs from/to the internal cache.
3. Certificate handling to retrieve/store public key certificate from/to the internal cache
4. PKM utilitiey functions, eg. obtain the distinguished name of the owner of the private key

PKM Facility relies on the Cryptographic Support Facility (CSF) for all cryptographic operations including the generation and storage of private keys.

Within the project framework, PKM APIs are not visible to outside of Star 's core services. For a full description on this topic, please refer to the SESAME V4 Public Key Management Application developers' guide.

The Cryptographic Support Facility

The SESAME Cryptographic Support Facility (CSF) is responsible for all cryptography related operation in the system, including generation and secure storage of cryptographic keys. The CSF implements plug-replaceable cryptographic algorithms hidden by a set of generic APIs covering both symmetric (secret key cryptography) and asymmetric (public key cryptography) technologies.

Since CSF is a trusted component in the security system, subject of export control in most countries, the use of its APIs has to be restricted to the intend of use and their keying information must not be available to unauthorized or untrusted code in conformance with the legislation of the local Authority.

CSF manages the following objects:

- cryptographic algorithms covering reversible (DES, RSA) and irreversible (Message Digest) algorithms
- the Quality of services (QOS) defines the use of cryptographic algorithms within a CSF area (domain). The QOS can be only managed by the CSF Administrator, it is composed of

  a service (integrity or privacy)

  a strength (weak , medium or strong)

---

24 for a complete set of GSS-APIs, please refer to the SESAME V4 GSS-API Application developers' Guide.

a n algorithm class (symmetric or asymmetric)

- Cryptographic keys covering secret and public keys, the generation and secure storage of those keys.
- CSF context, an opaque structure, which has to be establish before able to execute any cryptographic operation. The CSF context holds informations referenced to key use, algorithm and the quality of service.

CSF APIs are provided in the following main groups:

1. APIs to initialise CSF module, must be invoked before any other operation. It includes the retrieve of defined system QOS.
2. APIs to generate keys for a given algoritm, e.g. generation of keys or derivation of a secret key from an input string or basic key.
3. APIs to handle keys independently of the way it is stored, e.g. initialise, release
4. APIs to manage cryptography context, e.g. initialisation, create, release, duplicate, ...
5. APIs to support information data's protection, e.g. encrypt, decrypt, generate/verify check value.
6. APIs to extract and restore cryptography contexts and their keys.

In addition to these APIs, SESAME CSF supplies a control program csfcp for administration of CSF data, e.g. QOS setup, CSF domain configuration, ...

CSF APIs however are used only within the Star security services and not visible to any other component or application. Please refer to the SESAME V4 Cryptographic Application developers' guide for more information on this topic.

5.6 Conclusions

The completion of the Business Analysis exercise for the Star satellites has enabled the identification of the potential demand for services of a common nature that could usefully be developed by the core project resources.

These common services are intended to act as a platform for the development of specific applications which would reflect the individual requirements of each satellite and its healthcare network environment. There are two clear areas that have been highlighted by the work:

- the primary/secondary care interface
- remote consultant-to-consultant co-operation

Addressing these areas with telematic services will go a long way towards providing a seamless service to the patient.

The *primary/secondary care interface* can be further classified into *administrative* functions (identifying services, booking appointments, etc.) and *clinical* functions (test results, viewing the EPR, etc.). The priorities attached to each of these areas by our users at the sites will guide the rest of the work in the project.

The common issue of security has to conform not only to European legislation (e.g. Directive 95/46/EC) but also to local requirements. Common services must be able to at least:

- precisely identify and authenticate the users of the systems
- restrict access to patient related information to:
  - duly authorised healthcare practitioners

- the patient
- authorities for very specific purposes, e.g. anonymised epidemiological data
- preserve the integrity of the patient related information and its production status (who, when, where, etc.)
- preserve the consistency and coherence of information, particularly when it is distributed
- preserve the data from loss whether by destruction or by unauthorised copies.

Various technologies are being investigated by the satellites to ensure the confidentiality, integrity and authentication of the users, including the use of smartcards and encryption/decryption mechanisms (e.g. digital signatures and public key encryption). The approach taken by Starwas to develop a number of services Star from which the satellites could choose. In the event the two main satellites did not implement the Star security service as defined since they did not have the SESAME platform.

Within the Intercare environment, the consortium is different and the demonstrator sites will still not have a SESAME environment. A different approach will be taken to develop role-based security functionality. This will be done using wherever possible by using security services from OMG (Object Management Group) in a role-based way down to the lowest practical level.

For more information about Star, Intercare and the developing security services contact:

Paul Cooper
Project Manager Star & Intercare
IMS, Sandymount, Station Road, Woburn Sands, MK17 8RR, UK
Phone: (IMS) +44-1908-588806 or (home office) +44-1279-466366
Email: pcooper@imsgrp.com or paul@mira.demon.co.uk
Web: http://www.imsgrp.com or http://www.mira.demon.co.uk

Case Studies of Security Problems and their Solutions
G.O. Klein (Ed.)
IOS Press, 2000

6. The TrustHealth Pilot Experiment in Danderyd Hospital

Birgitta Wilson Claréus

6.1 Abstract

The Danderyd Hospital has implemented the use of a security system using smart cards held by all 4500 users of the extensive information systems used for administrative tasks as well as medical records. The system is using RSA based public key encryption and separate security servers for authorisation control. An analysis of costs and benefits is provided in this chapter.

6.2 Introduction to the project

The TrustHealth 1 project was a project within the Health Telematics sector of the European Commission 4th framework programme Telematics Applications. The project aimed to facilitate the establishment of trustworthy information systems in health care by providing:

- A set of specifications for security services and interfaces.
- A trusted third party service infrastructure with operational systems in some countries and publicly available specifications.

The project brought together users, research institutions, providers of security technology and health care applications with infrastructure service providers.

The TrustHealth 1 project had no resources available for actual implementation of the security specifications in actual healthcare applications but the project was fortunate to include the Danderyd Hospital where a decision was taken to implement a full scale security system based on the principles published by the TrustHealth project. For more information about TrustHealth see www.ehto.be/projects/trusthealth.

6.3 Organisations Involved

The partners involved in the Swedish trial were Danderyds Hospital, outside of Stockholm, AU-Systems (this part of AU-Systems is now ID2-technologies) as a TTP-systems provider, Dynasoft (this is now Security Dynamics Sweden) as a security tool-kit provider and Siemens as a provider of an Electronic Healthcare record system. SPRI was responsible for conducting an evaluation study.

6.4 The Danderyd System

6.4.1 The hospital and its information system

The Danderyd Hospital is a large hospital in Northern Stockholm with 4200 in the staff and some 100 medical students. In addition another 1000 are working in the surrounding North-Eastern healthcare area are part of the same IT security solution including primary care centres, Psychiatry and a Geriatric clinic. From 1993 the Hospital has started to implement an Electronic Healthcare record system that in mid 1997 covered all hospital clinics. This is the Melior system provided by Siemens Health Services.

The hospital is also using a system for Patient Administration called VAS supplied by Cap Programmator (Cap Gemeni Sogeti Group of Sweden) that is also used throughout the hospital.

The hospital management decided early on that security was an extremely important issue and the IT department was instructed to find the best available solution that would also meet the demand of easy use with a request for a single log-on procedure in this multi-server, multi application environment.

After a study of available possibilities it was already in 1994 decided that the solution had to be built on a RSA based solution with smart cards. The security project started before the TrustHealth project but was later included and the extensive experiences of a full scale implementation has been made available for the European project.

6.4.2 Overview of the security solution

The security system at Danderyd's Hospital is based on a user smart card with RSA and two private keys. One key is for authentication and encryption and the other is for digital signatures. The local workstation uses a software called AVI-BoKS in the PC provided by AU-systems and a server security package including authorisation administration from Dynasoft (now part of Security Dynamics) kalled BoKS.

This system allows for a local protection of the PC hard disk using encryption and a single user authentication of the user with his smart card. When using the network resources an automatic process is started with a challenge response authentication to the Security Server running BoKS. When a specific application is selected such as the Healthcare Record System, Melior, the user just clicks on an ICON and the specific server is accessed and in contact with the security server a similar challenge response procedure is performed authenticating the user and in some cases also establishing a confidentiality protected encrypted link. The OS of the database server will then parse the authenticated identity of the user to the Application software. When a card needs to be revocated this could easily be done in the central security master server. This server was in the first phase not using X.509 directory structure but a propiretary database.

6.5 The organisation of card and certificate issuing

In the case of Danderyd Hospital it was decided to operate the issuing of cards and certificates locally at the premises with its own staff. This decision was based on the fact that at the time of decision there were no public services available. The setting up and operation of such an internal TTP-service proved to be quite expensive but many important lessons were learned.

In the first pilot phase, the IT department was acting as a card issuer. Later it was decided that the hospital security unit would operate the service. In the new organisation the security unit is responsible for both physical security and information security.

A room with appropriate physical security using special locks, alarm and a safe was prepared and a staff of two persons were trained and allocated the task of being card issuers.

In addition to the function of the smart card as an electronic security device, Danderyd Hospital decided to have photographs on the Healthcare professional cards and to use the cards as visible badges in most areas.

We have defined written instructions for all aspects of the registration of new users and the procedure of issuing and revoking cards.
The process can be summarised follows:

1) The local security administrator in the clinical department prepares a requisition form for a card and user rights in the computer applications for a specific employee.
2) The responsible head of the clinical department signs the request form.
3) An appointment to the security department card issuing unit is made.
4) At a visit a digital photo is taken and the personal data on the request form is compared with the separate personnel database maintained by Security based on information from the personnel department.
5) The security staff enters the data on the working place and authorisation of the applicant and starts the software to issue a card and certificate.
6) A Certificate is generated and private keys and other data are recorded on the smart card.
7) The digital photo is printed on the card in the same device.
8) An initial PIN code is printed and given to the card holder.
9) The written instructions for the card holder are explained and the person is asked to try the card in a special PC for this purpose. In this process they are also asked to change the initial PIN code supplied to something the staff can not see and which is not recorded in the system.
10) The Card holder/new user is returning to his local security administrator who enters his access rights in the appropriate applications.

6.6 Evaluation usability/functionality

The IT department is quite content with the installed system and the easier **security administration**. Previously 2–3 persons were involved providing new passwords and user names.

The security department staff concluded that after one year all routines worked well.

The security department concluded that after a number of initial problems everything now worked fine.

The users were asked a number of questions in a questionaire to 50 users in three different departments. 80% answered.

30% reported that they were helped by the card while 14% reported the card to be a burden. The rest felt nothing in particular. However, the staff is generally well aware of the increased security.

6.7 Analysis of costs and benefits

The analysis provided herein should not be taken as exact but give a good indication of the types of costs and their magnitude. It should be emphasised that the reported costs here are relevant for the context in which this was the first large scale pilot of this kind and when the hospital decided to build its own Certification authority/"TTP".

The following types of costs were separated:

Planning and development	
Requirement analysis, Evaluation and Negotiation with suppliers, Tests, Hospital staff	17 man months
Supplier development, software and equipment including cards	0.5 MECU
Education of key personnel	
Security unit	6 man months
IT-department	10 days
The Systems administrators at the different clinics	40 x 1 day
Implementation at the different clinics 6000 employees, 2500 PCs and smart card readers	
IT-department	8 man months
Security Unit	12 man months
The System administrators in the clinics	36 man months
The staff	48–60 man months
Operation	
IT-department	6 man months
Security Unit	18 man months
Systems administrators	8 man months
Staff	no additional work

The total costs for development, and introduction of the advanced security system was thus estimated to be 11 MSEK = 1,3 MECU. This should then be compared with 6000 individual card users and 2500 PCs. The cost per person was thus 217 ecu.

6.7.1 The profits

A direct gain in less time used for administration of the old type of security system with passwords estimated at 24 man months. A larger factor was the shorter time required for log-on of each user at each occasion. This was estimated to be 10 seconds faster per log-on/ ten times a day. This adds up to 48 man months for the 6000 in the staff.

6.8 Conclusions

The new security system was considered to be a major gain in the security level achieved with all applications and the cryptographic advanced security was considered a prerequisite for introducing an Electronic Healthcare Record system in this hospital.

The users generally accepted the system well and the facilitated single log-on to all the different applications in the complex server environment was a major gain.

This together with the facilitated security administration was estimated to save a total of 6 man years every year in this scale (6000 users).

It was also clear that the costs for actually introducing the system (purchasing) as well as issuing of cards and certificates became higher in this pilot situation than it should be for another healthcare organisation which could probably do it for less than 50%.

The conclusion of running its own certification authority was rather negative. It costs quite a lot and requires a lot of training an availability of specialised staff. If public services from e.g. Sweden Post would have been available the hospital would have preferred such a solution according to the head of the IT department.

7. Security Infrastructure for a Regional Electronic Medical Record

Bernd Blobel and Peter Pharow

7.1 Abstract

This chapter looks at the security infrastructure around a regional electronic medical record. It considers first the generic security model and then the specific case study of the Regional Cancer Register in Magdeburg/Saxony Anhalt which was part of the TrustHealth 1 project.

7.2 Introduction

All developed countries around the world are concerned with the change of their healthcare systems towards a shared care architecture. This development is caused by the well-known requirements for higher efficiency and quality of the care provided. Shared care in modern healthcare systems in the sense of "a continuous and co-ordinated activity of different persons in different institutions under the employment of different methods at different times in order to be able to help patients optimally with respect to their medical, psychological and social being" demands also the sharing of the information systems involved. As a result, these communicating and co-operating information systems form different types of electronic medical record architectures, dealing with personal medical, i.e. usually very sensitive, data. Increasingly, the communication and co-operation between the systems, nowadays provided by middleware approaches and called "systems' interoperability", is crossing organisational, regional or in the future even national boundaries (Blobel 1997c; Blobel and Holena, 1997a). Such open interoperable information systems are exposed to a variety of attacks and, therefore, very vulnerable. Thus, such information systems require appropriate solutions guaranteeing security, safety, and quality of data and procedures provided by the systems. In the paper presented, the concepts of safety and quality are not considered.

7.3 Generic Security Model

Looking for security in health information systems, we have to respond to two kinds of challenges. Firstly, based on the general security model (Figure 1) already published in several papers, the security services, needed to protect such systems against the security threats and risks they are exposed to, must be specified. The model distinguishes between communication security and application security. Thus, it allows the focus on the specific part, e.g., on communication security in the case of security enhanced Electronic Data

Interchange (EDI) like HL7[25], EDIFACT[26], and xDT[27], or on application security to improve authorisation and access control including the definition of roles for decision support.

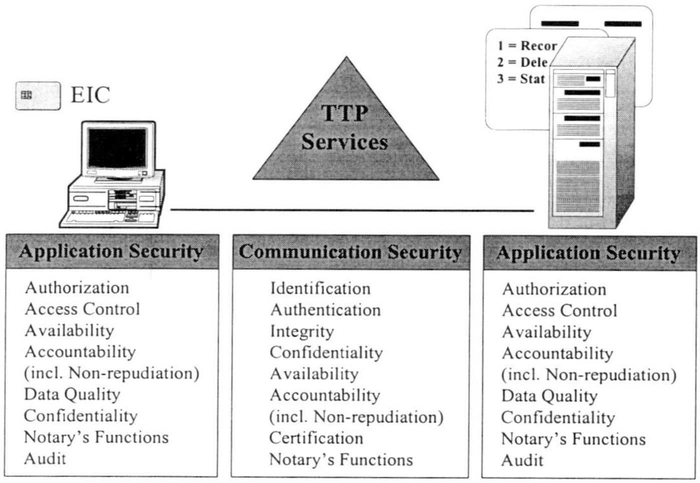

Figure 1: General Security Model.

Secondly, medical and afterwards security-related use cases (scenarios) must be specified to select sets of security services as well as sets of security mechanisms providing these services needed in the context of the special medical and security-related use cases (Blobel and Roger-France, 1998). The consideration can be refined by the higher granularity of algorithms and data, facilitating the implementers' view.

The security services defined provide the link between the security requirements and objectives as described in a security policy, and the security mechanisms and management to satisfy these requirements (The SEISMED consortium, 1997). The former concerns the medical end user, the latter concerns system administrators.

7.4 Security Domains

Increasingly, the distributed architecture of shared care information systems is based on networks. Due to their user friendliness, the use of standardised user interfaces, tools, and protocols and therefore their platform independence, the number of really open information systems based on the Internet or Intranets (corporate networks, virtual private networks) has been growing during the last couple of years (Blobel and Katsikas, 1998).

---

25 Health Industry Level 7 Interface Standard

26 EDI for Administration, Commerce and Transport

27 German protocols for EDI between doctors' office computer systems as well as between them and other providers' information systems.

To keep systems and their security behaviour manageable, organisational, logical, and technical components are grouped into domains as, e.g., policy domains (Blobel, 1997b; Blobel and Holena, 1997b). Forming such a domain of agreed security policy (Figure 2), the domain is considered to need only a special protection to other domains with their own policy or to policy-free domains as the Internet, e.g. using firewalls or proxy servers. Thereby the internal domain is assumed as secure, often neglecting internal threats and attacks. Most of the security services currently available are based on system authentication (Kerberos, IPSec ...) (Blobel and Katsikas, 1998; Katsikas, Spinellis, 1998). Regarding the specific requirements and conditions of healthcare, the underlying security model must consider the whole spectre of security services and mechanisms. Thus finally, a more realistic concept is that of secure micro domains only (Blobel and Holena, 1997b). The domain concept including common middleware approaches is explained in detail, e.g., in (Blobel, Bleumer, 1997).

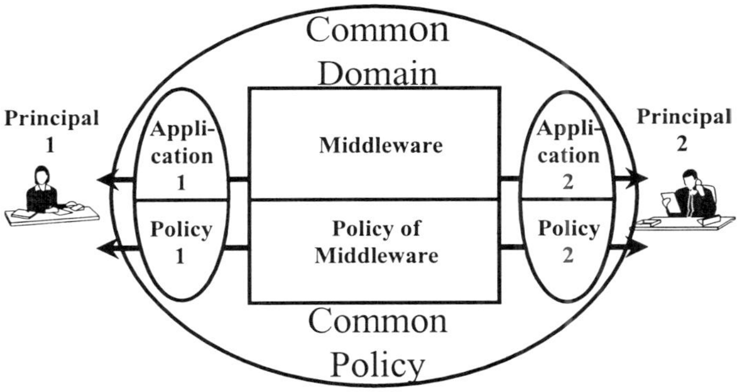

Figure 2: Policy Bridging.

The specific legal, social and psychological conditions of healthcare require person related security services as demonstrated in (Blobel, 1998). The need for strong user authentication is true for all business which requires accountability (and audit) for legal or ethical reasons. Additionally, the demand of user authentication in healthcare is caused to fulfil the "need to know" principle, to accept the privacy of patient's information, to bind information to the care purpose, and to facilitate the trusting doctor-patient relationship. Therefore in Europe, but increasingly also in other regions of the world, security tokens as individual and/or professional smart cards (chip cards with crypto controller), in the future combined with biometric measures, have been introduced. They keep private keys and provide security services as authentication, digital signature, and key encipherment. In CEN TC 251, several security services and mechanisms, protocols, cards and card readers, as well as principles and tools of the security infrastructure like TTP services are currently under standardisation (The TRUSTHEALTH Consortium, 1997).

7.5 The Regional Cancer Register Magdeburg/Saxony-Anhalt

The care of cancer patients is a long-standing example of shared care. As an integrated clinical cancer documentation system, the Regional Clinical Cancer Register Magdeburg/Saxony-Anhalt was the first distributed interoperable regional healthcare information system in Germany. The highly sensitive content of the Clinical Cancer Register information and the open system architecture used are demanding a high level of security, reliability, and privacy of data records and communication procedures (Blobel, 1996a). Based on results of several projects related to security in healthcare and funded by the European Commission (Blobel and Pharow, 1998), the security solutions for the type of systems mentioned will be discussed in the paper.

As an Electronic Health Record (EHR) in oncology, the Clinical Cancer Register of Magdeburg/Saxony-Anhalt was implemented to improve quality and efficiency of cancer care including quality assurance, to facilitate research and education, and to improve communication and co-operation between the involved health professionals (Blobel, 1996a, 1997a). For a catchment area with more than 1.2 million inhabitants, currently an increasing number of the 58 partner clinics and the Oncological Follow-up Organisation Centre[28] are on-line connected to an extended patient-centred and case-oriented tumour documentation covering all essential information with a range from cancer diagnosis up to conclusion of the case.

The Medical Informatics Department at the University Hospital of Magdeburg is hosting and maintaining the registry server. It also contributes to the further development of the ORACLE-based registry application called "Giessener Tumordokumentationssystem" (GTDS) and developed by the University of Giessen, Germany, applying ORACLE tools as forms, reports etc.

In 1993, the Clinical Cancer Register Magdeburg was the first German healthcare application with advanced security mechanisms ensuring strong authentication of users as well as integrity and confidentiality of exchanged data using the MACS (Modem Access Control System) for analogue line, the Kryptoguard LAN L3 boxes for ISDN lines between the secure server and secure external LAN (closed systems), and the ISDN Kryptoguard PC plug-in card for stand-alone (secure) PCs connected to the (secure) server by ISDN lines. Improvement and further development of the system was and is embedded in several regional, national, and European projects, related to both security (e.g. ISHTAR, TrustHealth, EUROMED-ETS, MEDSEC) and architecture (e.g. HANSA) and funded by the European Union. The registry system was set up as a centralised architecture with PC clients under terminal emulation. Currently, step by step the application system get improved developing and testing client-server architecture up to independent interoperable systems partly based upon means of middleware concepts as, e.g., CORBA[29] and HL7[30] (see for reference e.g. Blobel, 1997a; Blobel and Holena, 1997a,b). The legal framework of cancer registries is very important as well but not issued in this paper. See for reference e.g. (Blobel, 1996a).

---

28 The Oncological Follow-up Organisation Centre facilitates the cancer care of GPs and specialised oncological practices.

29 Common Object Request Broker Architecture, the strictly object-oriented middleware approach of the Object Management Group (OMG, 1995).

30 Health Level Seven Information Interchange Protocol.

The TrustHealth-1 project[31] (The TRUSTHEALTH Consortium, 1997) aimed to facilitate the establishment of trustworthy information systems in healthcare, providing a certain set of specifications for security services and interfaces by publicly available specifications as well as a trusted third party service infrastructure with operational systems in some European countries. The shared care requirements mentioned above had to be fulfilled, accepting PC type workstations as nowadays dominating clients. The need to control key and certificate distribution made a smart card format ideal. Thus, the Health Professional Card (HPC) was born.

7.6 Health Professional Cards

According to the Telematics Initiative of the German federal state of Saxony-Anhalt providing a distributed oncological Electronic Health Record (EHR) (Blobel, 1996c) and following the TrustHealth-1 specifications, the first HPC was introduced in May 1997. The card is used as a secure token to store secret keys for authentication, digital signature, and encryption purposes as well as to store other items as administrative data. It was designed to be implemented in several existing card configurations avoiding the need to create new masks and can be implemented on several existing card operating systems.

Right from the beginning, the HPC specification follows available and applicable ISO 7816-x standards, and supports symmetric (DES) and asymmetric (RSA) cryptographic algorithms. In the Magdeburg version (TRM.HPC) it has to keep several different secret keys separating the key for the digital signature service from that for authentication, symmetric key encipherment and other services, e.g. to allow different key lengths and different times of validity. One separate key may serves as some kind of class key (profession group) enabling authorised access to encrypted data in archives in terms of impersonal referral or for emergency cases. Optionally, the card may contain a symmetric key used for interaction with a patient data card and data for other applications, e.g access privileges used for local computer protection. Figure 4 shows the HPC in a functional context. A more detailed description can be found in (The TRUSTHEALTH Consortium, 1997).

Only with a correct PIN (the next generations of card will include biometrical algorithms) the host computer requests the user's authentication certificate from the directory service. It verifies the certificate, extracts the user's public key, and sends a challenge including a random number and preferably a time stamp or pre-defined pattern to the card. The card transforms the random number with the secret key and sends it back for verification. The host computer verifies the response with the public key stored in the certificate. The public keys of a user, together with some other information, rendered unforgeable by encipherment with the secret key of the certification authority which issued it. The authentication process may be repeated at regular intervals, or every time a critical operation is to be performed. For details see (Blobel, Spiegel, 1998a,b).

---

31 The TrustHealth-1 project was strongly co-ordinated with the German Model Trail "Health Professional Cards" (HPC) employing HPC for strong and certified authentication and TTP communication security services (Arbeitskreis, 1996). The demonstrated solution is part of this project.

7.7 Security Toolkits

A specific security toolkit "SecuDE (Security Development Environment)" acts as an intelligent interface between the card infrastructure and the application, and provides implementation support and security services as origin authentication, data integrity, non-repudiation of origin, and data confidentiality using symmetric (e.g. DES, 3DES, IDEA) and asymmetric (e.g. RSA, DSA, DSS) cryptographic algorithms as well as various hash functions (e.g. MD4, MD5, SHA), by this way realising a Personal Security Environment (PSE). The toolkit is currently under further development to include new algorithms and libraries. SecuDE is able to handle X.509 public key certification functionalities, certification paths, cross certification, and certificate revocation. It provides utilities and library functions for the operation of certification authorities (CA) and interaction between a certifying CA and its certified users. For more see (The TRUSTHEALTH Consortium, 1997).

7.8 Trusted Third Party Services

A Trusted Third Party (TTP) provides all services required for a trustworthy health telematics infrastructure. Mirroring the well-known paper-based "real" world, in the legal sense a TTP has to provide at least the same level of confidence and reliability within an "electronic" world as it is required for paper documents (see Figure 6). A detailed model including functional roles and their interaction within a TTP infrastructure is described in (The TRUSTHEALTH Consortium, 1997).

Formally, a TTP may not be connected with any of the communicating parties but independent, thus can be trusted to provide the infrastructural and value added security services in a secure and trustworthy manner. It comprises all of the independent organisations offering security services. To fulfil its basic objective offering security services with the necessary degree of (technical and business including policy) functionality and assurance, the TTP has to provide a secure IT and communication system. Responsible for the defined services, its formal or legal position within its service domain might be equally important.

TTPs establish several trusted authorities providing different TTP services. To identify the principals in a security domain unambiguously a Naming Authority (NA) is needed. The unique name has to be provided to both the Public Key Registration Authority (PK-RA) and the Public Key Certification Authority (PK-CA) to be linked to certificates. The profession relationship aimed to the electronic identity card has to be ensured by Professional Registration Authorities (Pr-RA) and Professional Certification Authorities (Pr-CA) respectively. The public keys of the principals as well as their certificates have to be published in a convenient way by an X.500 based Directory Services (DS). To join the directories with the secure environment provided by the security toolkit, an interface (LDAP, DAP) must be used. Figure 3 presents the general TTP roles or services and a possible interaction model.

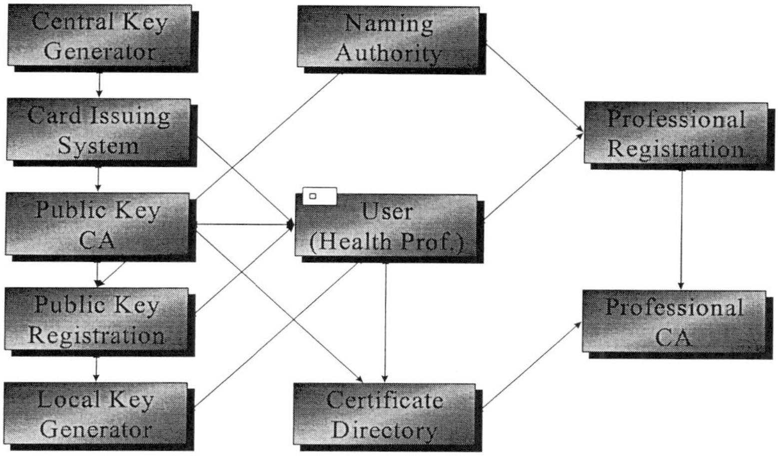

Figure 3: TTP roles and possible interaction model.

There are common views and requirements to TTP infrastructures but also healthcare specific needs of partial functionalities and security requirements depending on the security policy in question. Nevertheless, looking for functional specifications of TTP services relevant for the healthcare sector, a few elements of relevant security policies in the European healthcare could be specified within the TrustHealth-1 (The TRUSTHEALTH Consortium, 1997) and the SIREN (see this volume) project. Examples of relevant issues would be the organisation and functioning of the public key and Pr-RAs and the interaction with directory services directly attaching to and influencing the acceptance of the users.

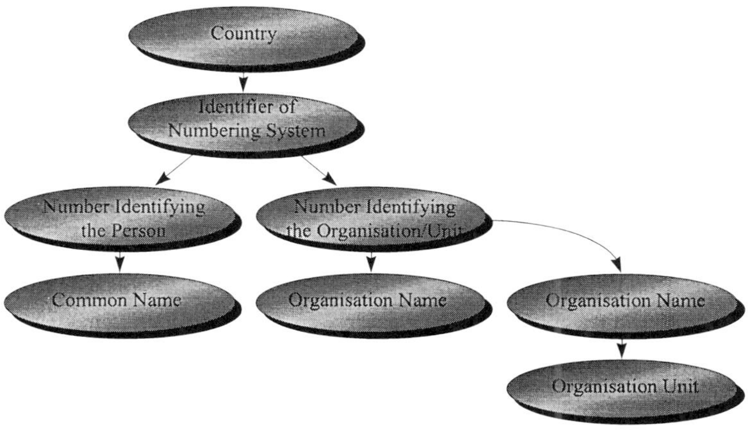

Figure 4: Naming Scheme.

The close relations between naming schemes of public key and professional certificates also gives specific requirements for the organisation and functioning of the naming authority (Figure 4). The concatenation of the attributes of each level results in the structure of a unique name.

It is desirable to have the professional certificate created by the same professional authority that delivers the valid professional information to be certified. Such professional or governmental organisations should represent the profession (including specialities, etc.) and must have a complete overview of all members of that profession in the TTP's catchment area. They should be competent to judge the status of each professional and have to dispose the unique registration number of each professional, if such a number exists. The professionals should be obliged to keep this organisation up-to-date concerning their professional status. Therefore, the TTP must have an appropriate legal status. It is mainly the professional registration that can be of importance for healthcare information systems. Thus, it is important to distinguish the general registration or license to practice from the qualifications given by educational degrees.

The technical structure of the X.500 Directory Service is based on the modern "client-server principle". The user's assistant is the "directory user agent" (DUA) — an application software component in the workplace computer — which facilitates user access to the Directory Service. The actual service itself is provided by the "directory system agent" (DSA) on a server computer.

7.9 Implementation of the Pilot

As a requirement and a basis for secure distributed interoperable EHR in oncology, the system-oriented security architecture of the Regional Clinical Cancer Register Magdeburg/Saxony-Anhalt will be improved introducing security services based upon the HPC and TTP services. Performing a feasibility study, in the first implementation phase only 10 HPC and 8 terminals have been implemented testing algorithms, protocols, and connections. The single-chip Philips 83C852 implemented on a STARCOS PK V.1.0 smartcard, and a STARCOS-related smartcard terminal ICT 800 according to the MCT (Multifunctional Card Terminal) specification have been used (Arbeitsgemeinschaft, 1996). After this first phase first results related to medium-scale and large scale user acceptability and performance will be achieved.

TTP employs X.509v3 certificates and X.500-based standard directories for distribution of certificates and revocation in the case of compromised or lost keys and cards respectively. The functionalities are handled in a cross-certified manner. The Physicians' Chambers of Saxony-Anhalt and Lower Saxony will provide this service. Regarding different security requirements depending on used services, mirrored (regularly updated) directories without any other TTP services could be provided on the application domain level, e.g. in the hospital. Currently the decentralised key generation favoured for trust reasons is often rejected due to the insecure users' PC environment and the rest probability of doubled keys.

Two different kinds of key-pairs each with a key-length of 512 bit are generated by SecuDE: one for the purpose of a digital signature application and one for the purpose of a key encipherment application. The algorithm used for signing is RSA with the MD5 hash function, the algorithm for key encipherment is also RSA. The corresponding PK-certificates are X.509v1-certificates. SecuDE is able to handle two X.509v1-certificates which are used for different purposes by an internal supported naming. X.509v3 certificates are scheduled for the second phase of the pilot.

The first security-related function which is realised during the first phase of the pilot is signing and encrypting of a number of bytes, which represent exported data of the GDTS-database. This enveloped data is then sent to the recipient via ftp. The recipient decrypts and verifies the received data. If the signature is correct the number of bytes are interpreted as a data set of the database and imported to its own GDTS-database.

More details concerning partners, responsibilities, dependencies of actions and processes, detailed specifications about interactions between client, server, terminal, and card can be found in (The TRUSTHEALTH Consortium, 1997) as well.

7.10 Conclusion

Combining and including the results of several security-related projects funded by the EU, as ISHTAR, EUROMED-ETS and others, the TrustHealth-1 specifications for security services, interfaces, and infrastructures can be used to design secure applications. HPC and TTP are able to provide security services and mechanisms, which can be used to realise distributed interoperable health information systems like EHR. On the one hand, further investigations, developments, and early implementations are directed to integrate the TrustHealth-1 security infrastructure based on HPC and TTP services also in middleware architectures (e.g. Blobel, 1997c; Blobel and Holena, 1997a,b). Shared care information systems are requiring such solutions issued by international or at least European standards. On the other hand, large field trials based on TrustHealth-1 results are required to prove the usability of HPC and related TTP in terms of awareness, usefulness, and user-friendliness. TrustHealth-2 will provide demonstration scenarios in six European countries including more than 1500 potential users. Human and legal aspects will play an important role within the long-term evaluation process. Common integration scenarios and standardised card specifications and security tool specifications to be used for the implementations in the different sites will allow a cross-border transmission of medical and administrative data using means as Internet, electronic mail, and secure file transfer. Last but not least it will be the basis that could lead to a pan-European TTP network as it was tested in EUROMED-ETS (Blobel and Katsikas, 1998, Katsikas, Spinellis, 1998).

Acknowledgement

The authors are in dept to the European Commission and to the Ministry of Education and Science of the German Federal State Saxony-Anhalt for funding as well as to the partners of the TrustHealth project, especially the GMD, for kind co-operation.

References

Arbeitsgemeinschaft (1996) AG "Karten im Gesundheitswesen", GMD-Forschungszentrum Informationstechnik GmbH: Multifunktionale KartenTerminals (MKT) für das Gesundheitswesen und andere Anwendungsgebiete. Spezifikation Version 1.0.

Arbeitskreis (1996) AK "Deutscher Modellversuch Health Professional Cards".

Blobel, B. (1996a) Clinical Record Systems in Oncology. Experiences and Developments on Cancer Registries in Eastern Germany. In: R. Anderson (edr.) Preproceedings of the International Workshop "Personal Information - Security, Engineering and Ethics" pp 37-54, Cambridge, 21-22 June, 1996, also published in Personal Medical Information - Security, Engineering, and Ethics (edr.), pp 39-56. Spinger, Berlin 1997.

Blobel, B. (1996b) A Regional Clinical Cancer Documentation System for an Optimal Shared Healthcare in Cancer. In: J. Brender, J.P. Christensen, J.-R. Scherrer and P. McNair (edrs.) Medical Informatics Europe '96, pp 1019-1026. IOS Press, Amsterdam.

Blobel, B. (1996c) Konzeption für Telematikanwendungen im Gesundheitswesen sowie für ältere und behinderte Menschen. Telematik-Initiative des Landes Sachsen-Anhalt. Magdeburg, 19. Februar 1996.

Blobel, B. (1997a) Object-oriented Middleware Architectures — Trends for Distributed Health Information Systems. Bulletin SSIM - SGMI No. 34, Juillet - Juli 1997, pp. 4-8.

Blobel, B. (1997b) Security Requirements and Solutions in Distributed Electronic Health Records. In: L. Yngström and J. Carlsen(edrs.) Information Security in Research and Business, pp 377-390. Chapman & Hall, London.

Blobel, B (1997c) Treats and Solutions for Data Protection and Data Security in Healthcare Information Systems. Toward An Electronic Patient Record (1997), Volume 5, Issue 8, pp 1-16.

Blobel, B. (1998) The Need and Practice of User Related Security and TTP Services in Middleware Systems. Proceedings of the Conference "Towards An Electronic Patient Record '98", Supplement, pp 34-40. May 9 - May 16, 1998, San Antonio.

Blobel, B., Bleumer, G., Müller, A., Flikkenschild, E. and Ottes, F. (1997) Current Security Issues Faced by Healthcare Establishments. Deliverable of the HC1028 Telematics Project ISHTAR, February 1997.

Blobel, B and Holena, M. (1997a) Comparing middleware concepts for advanced healthcare system architectures. International Journal of Medical Informatics 46 (1997) pp. 69-85.

Blobel, B. and Holena, M. (1997b) Security Threats and Solutions in Distributed, Interoperable Health Information Systems Using Middleware. In: J. Dudeck, B. Blobel, W. Lordieck and T. Bürkle (edrs.) New Technologies in Hospital Information Systems, pp. 66-73. IOS Press, Amsterdam.

Blobel, B. and Katsikas, S.K. (1998) Patient data and the Internet — security issues Chairpersons' introduction. International Journal of Medical Informatics 49 (1998) pp. S5-S8.

Blobel, B. and Pharow, P. (1998) Results of European Projects Improving Security of Distributed Health Information Systems. In: B. Cesnik, A.T. McCray, J.-R. Scherrer (edrs.) MEDINFO '98, pp. 1119-1123. IOS Press Amsterdam, Berlin, Oxford, Tokyo, Washington DC.

Blobel, B. and Roger-France, F. (1998) Healthcare Security View Based on the Security Services Concept. ISHTAR Project HC 1028, Deliverable, August 1998.

Blobel, B., Spiegel, V., Krohn, R., Pharow, P., Engel, K. (1998a) Standard Guide for HL7 Communication Security. ISIS MEDSEC Project, Deliverable 30, August 1998.

Blobel, B., Spiegel, V., Krohn, R., Pharow, P., Engel, K. (1998b) Standard Guide for Implementing EDI Communication Security. ISIS MEDSEC Project, Deliverable 31, August 1998.

Katsikas, S.K., Spinellis, D.D., Iliadis, J., Blobel, B. (1998) Using Trusted Third Parties for secure telemedical applications over the WWW: The EUROMED-ETS approach. International Journal of Medical Informatics 49 (1998) pp. 59-68.

OMG (1995) The CORBA Security Specification. OMG Doc.No. 95-12-01.

The SEISMED Consortium (edr.) (1996) Data Security for Healthcare, Volume I-III. IOS Press, Amsterdam.

The TRUSTHEALTH Consortium (edr.) (1997) Trustworthy Health Telematics 1 project: Project Deliverables, 1996-1997.

8. Security and the RHINE Project

Albert van der Werff and Hubert Mensch

8.1 Abstract

This chapter provides an introduction to the RHINE project, and looks at the role of security and the need to implement a security policy within the regional environment.

8.2 Introduction to RHINE (Regional Health Information Networks in Europe)

In RHINE a representative group of Regions has decided to collaborate on a trans-European basis in order to improve health and patient care, and to increase quality of care and performance by reforming their health systems through the application of 'Information Technologies' (IT). In this respect 'Technologies for Business Processes' (TBP) are applied which focus on the improvement of healthcare and healthcare processes, as well as of administrative and managerial processes by IT.

Technologies for Business Processes recognise that implementation of information systems is 'not just about installing computers', but rather is concerned 'with changing the whole organisation', with implications for everyone working within it. While IT cannot reform the system, healthcare cannot be reformed without it. Management of change is a key issue both to successful implementation and to obtaining value from IT investments.

This joint initiative of the European Regions is called 'RHINE', which is an acronym for Regional Health Information Networks in Europe, symbolising through the reference to the name of the river, the evolution towards European unification. The RHINE-Initiative should be considered within the context of Article 129 of the Treaty of the European Union 1992, and related programmes of Community action in the field of health information and communication. The initiative is supported by the European Commission.

A first step to achieve its objectives is a General Accompanying Measure, called RHINE AM, aiming at the creation of awareness about the availability and benefits of advanced information technologies (IT), for:

- the improvement of efficiency and effectiveness of administration and management in public health and healthcare at regional level, and
- the establishment of an on-going European Forum of the European Regions for exchange of knowledge and support to IT users.

RHINE AM is initiated by a core group of five Regions, consisting of:

- North-Rhine Westphalia, Germany: Co-ordinating Partner
- Northern Greece, Greece
- Lombardia, Italy
- Stockholm County, Sweden
- Wales, United Kingdom

These Regions represent the different categories of health systems of Europe, both tax-based and insurance-based systems. The 2-year project (1997-1998) is co-funded by the European Commission DGIII/ESPRIT, and is registered under Nr 22669.

8.3 RHINE and security

One of the key common concerns in the project is Security and confidentiality. Personal health information is highly sensitive to a large extent. Without proper control, and legislation, information stored in computerised information management systems is more readily accessible to outsiders than the same information stored in manual filing systems, and linkages between computerised records for the same person can be more easily established. This development has increased public and professional concerns with regard to security and confidentiality. It is in particular important to protect information that is exchanged in open information systems and networks. Security of information and communication systems is generally defined as the combined set of three measures to preserve:

- Confidentiality: the prevention of the unauthorised disclosure of information;
- Integrity: the prevention of unauthorised modification of information;
- Availability: the prevention of unauthorised witholding of information or resources.

When paper as a bearer of information is substituted by electronic media in the health sector the legal arrangements and protection mechanisms may become inadequate. Uncertainty arises regarding acceptability and security of new technical solutions as e.g. electronic signatures as well as the proper legal treatment of these new approaches. Stimulated by the OECD, and the Commission of the European Union a rapid legislative development to cope with digital information has been initiated in Europe, but the results are still not satisfactory and a lot of work still has to be done.

Successful implementation of an Electronic Health Information Service is dependent upon security and confidentiality. The administrative top and senior management of a Region must accept full responsibility for ensuring the security and confidentiality of data. A clearly defined policy is needed as a platform for adequate measures with regard to security and data protection. Such a policy should take into account and respectively adopt formal and legal standards in this field as well as international directives of the Commission of the European Union and national legislation. The adopted security policy should be brought to the attention of all parties concerned within a Region, and refer to all components of an entire Electronic Regional Health Information System.

8.4 Implementation of the security policy

Within the RHINE AM, The project is investigating the generic security solutions which are required by the regional process types. However sensitive data are handled and the attention paid to security will strongly depend on the national or regional regulation. RHINE AM seeks to identify the common requirements which could be a starting basis agreed by the regions:

- formalise their security policy in terms of management and implementation
- propose the framework which allows to control and secure flows of information between the partners of the regional information system
- provide guidelines for partners to connect their own information system and maintain their connection in respect with the security requirements.

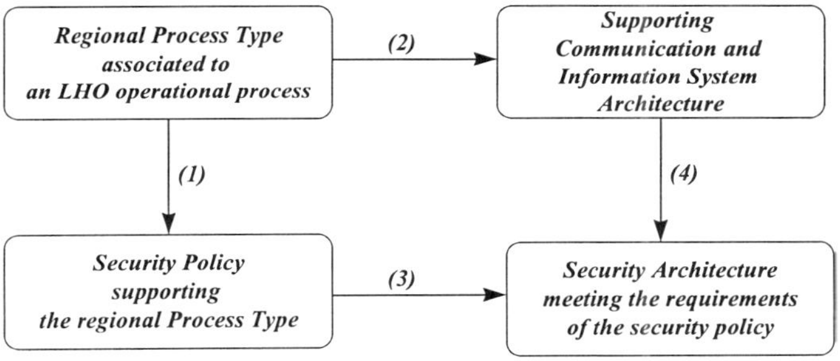

The security policy is one of the business process characteristics. It has to be defined for the regional processes according to the country regulation and regional context in order to design a security architecture.

The RHINE AM proposes the reference architecture of the communication and information system which supports each of regional process types.

The security policy is implemented through a security architecture meeting the requirements for:

- confidentiality
- integrity
- availability

Finally the security architecture must take place as a part of the overall architecture of the communication and information system.

Security policy

The RHINE AM has two ways to tackle the security issues related to the regional processes, the LHO operational processes being left outside the scope of the project:

- by considering common security policy for the administrative sectors
- by analysing the individual security requirements for each process element of each regional process type associated to a LHO operational process.

8.4.1.1 Common security policy for the administrative sectors

The health sector is split into 2 parts:

- a part which is controlled, in a given country, by the security rules common to all the administrative sectors. The regional processes within the health providers management domain can be seen in it. These common rules are left outside the scope of the RHINE AM, as being defined by a internal administrative sector body.
- the second part on which the RHINE AM concentrates and which is related to the sensitive information on the patients and the professionals.

8.4.1.2 Security requirements for sensible process elements

The security policy is defined for each process element of each process type associated to a LHO operational process. Within each regional process type, the security requirements attached to each process element are indeed quite different : integrity and availability for the Disseminating instruction process element, confidentiality and integrity for the Receiving reported information one. This approach leads to consider a large number of cases, and a third mixed approach looks better.

8.4.1.3 Focus on the process elements involving the identified patient

One can draw a matrix like the joint one for each operational process in the LHO. The number in the cells shows the order of the process element enactment within the regional process type.

The example is related to the caring process. The deep grey cells are concerned by security requirements because dealing with individual patient identified information.

Process Types / Process elements	Reporting	Supervision	Dissemination	Authorisation	X-Monitoring	Globalisation
Disseminating instruction towards LHO	(1)	(2)	(1)	(1)	(1)	(1)
Receiving reported information	(2)	(3)			(2)	
Disseminating information towards LHO	(3)		(3)			
Informing addressees	(4)	(4)		(4)	(3)	
Receiving instruction from upper level		(1)				
Receiving information from LHO			(2)	(2)		(2)
Sending answer to LHO				(3)		(3)

We will concentrate in the following example on the *Receiving reported information* in the *Reporting* process type, corresponding to the architecture discussed in the previous section.

Note: Considering the transfer of billing information to the sickness fund, a similar *Reporting Process*, but associated to the *reimbursement process*, can be enacted.

8.4.2 Security requirements for Receiving reported information process element

The objective of the Reporting Process associated to the operational caring process is to set up and maintain a regional cases base in which episodes are reconstructed from encounter or activity reports provided by different LHOs. It is required the reported individual information to be:

- sent by a recognised and authorised professionals at the LHO level,
- transferred through the regional network while the message integrity is preserved
- de-identified as regards to the patient, LHO and HCP identifiers
- added to the already anonymised existing case record

8.4.2.1 At the LHO level

The LHO information system is assumed to be protected against external unauthorised disclosure on connection (it is outside the scope of the RHINE AM). The LHO information system is interfaced with the regional reporting system in a way the reported information is presented in a HISA compliant format. The sensible information is identified under the patient's and providers' identifiers.

It is required:
- from the messages addresses at the regional level to provide assurance that they hold the claimed identity
- the LHO provides assurance it has, as source of data, the claimed identity

8.4.2.2 Network

Between the LHO interface and the regional repository, the network provides integrity of the messages, preventing their content to be
- consulted by an unauthorised party. The requirement can be met from the LHO only up to the de-identification component, the obtained anonymous information being of less interest for unauthorised party.
- altered, modified inserted or cancelled. This requirement has to be met from the LHO up to the regional repository

8.4.2.3 At the regional repository level

The repository itself is protected against unauthorised access to the resources. In addition, audit trail of the accesses can be set up.

But the main issue is the de-identification process which has to map a real identifier or a real identity to a single anonymous identifier, each time a new report is provided by the

LHO level. As the report can be provided by different LHOs, we have different situations, amongst others:
- There is no regional patients register and providers directory. The domain of the patient identifiers is then limited to each LHO. To obtain a single anonymous identifier, we can:
  - process the **constant** selected information of the messages,
  - require from each LHO a chaining with the identifier assigned by the previous visited LHO.
- There is a regional (or national) patient register, and the patient has an unique permanent identifier which can be mapped to an anonymous one by a trusted partner of the system.

The anonymisation problem is not yet completely solved. It is subject of several on-going developments and the different expected or existing solutions are depending on the requirements: is it necessary to chain or not the de-identified information? Is it needed to come back from the de-identified information to the identified one? Etc. In the RHINE project, which is an accompanying measure we have first to clearly express the requirements concerning the different process types within the national or regional context.

8.5 Conclusions

Security is one of the key common concerns within the project. The implementation of effective regional health information networks is dependent on the provision of security and confidentiality services. This is not the prime concern at regional levels but a clearly defined policy is needed based on a formal and legal standard as well directives from European and national level.

The RHINE project looks externally for this security infrastructure which can provide the basis for a clear and implementable policy in this area. It continues to look at the regional requirements which will form the process base for infrastructure policy in this context.

References

RHINE AM, Deliverable WP3/4 December 1997, LÖGD presenting in a section Enabling and Constraining Factors the security requirements applicable to the regions: Stockholm County; Wales; North Rhine Westphaly; Lombardy; Northern Greece.

RHINE AM, Deliverable WP5: RTD Analysis, December 1997, LÖGD.

ISO 7498: Information Technology - Open Systems Interconnection; Part 1: Basic Reference Model; Part 2: Security Architecture.

TrustHealth 1, Project HC1051, Deliverable D2.1, Selection of Security Services, 29 07 96, SPRI.

EHCRA, prENV12265, Electronic Health Care Record - Architecture, CEN/TC251, 1996.

HISA, ENV 12967-1, Health Information System Architecture, CEN/TC251, 1998.

For further information, please contact:

Dr. Albert van der Werff, The SOCRATES Network
E-mail: avdwsocr@wxs.nl

9. The TIDDM Project and Security

C. Mossa, A. Riva and R. Bellazzi

9.1 Abstract

This chapter looks at the project TIDDM and its experience in the area of security. It consists of an introduction to the project and an explanation of its context with Telemedicine. The chapter then describes the support architecture, the servers, protocol and the development environment. It identifies the TIDDM needs in the security area and provides an overview of security and cryptography solutions leading to an explanation of the implementation in TIDDM.

9.2 An introduction to the T-IDDM project

The T-IDDM project is designed to meet the needs of patients and physicians in Insulin Dependent Diabetes Mellitus (IDDM) care, and its methodology therefore lies on a careful analysis of current medical practice.

Conventional therapy of IDDM out-patients involves subcutaneous administration of exogenous insulin two to four times a day, self-monitoring of Blood Glucose levels, and insulin dose adjustment on the basis of the actual measurement, following individualized control tables defined by the physician. The results of self-monitoring are usually reported on a patient's diary.

Patients are periodically visited by physicians, in order to assess the insulin schedule and the total amount of daily insulin, on the basis of the metabolic control achieved. The metabolic control is usually evaluated by observing blood glucose measurements and the hypoglycemic events reported on the diaries (instant markers) as well as other important measurements, like Hb1A or glycosuria (period markers).

A typical scenario of IDDM management involves two main actors: an outpatient and a physician; the patient is visited by a diabetologist every two or three months; in the period between visits, the patient has responsibility for the self-management of his/her metabolic control. Unfortunately, a number of problems may occur during this period. Hypoglicemia or hyperglycemia episodes may happen, due to both wrong therapy implementations and metabolic instability causes, like other intercurrent diseases or stress periods. In this cases, the physician is required to assist the patient with telephone consultations, or to schedule an additionally visit; in the worst case a short period of hospitalization is needed. Metabolic instability episodes are often detected with a considerable delay since their onset. In a typical home monitoring setting, the patient must report the Blood Glucose Levels (BGL) measurements as well as the insulin dosages in a diary. The information contained in the diary must be checked and analyzed by the physician during each periodic visit. Such analysis is often difficult to perform, since the data are hand-written, and do not allow an easy statistical elaboration. Furthermore, when the physician is able to detect an episode in the past history (e.g. hyperglicemia), often the patient does not remember if there were specific reasons for that (e.g. an extra-meal intake). A large amount of the information contained in the diary is hence lost, due to the inefficiency of the data storage and retrieval.

On the basis of the above scenario analysis, the system proposed in the T-IDDM project will be based on two main components, a Patient Unit (PU), a Medical Unit (MU), connected in a Telemedicine Information System (TIS): patients and physicians will be hence provided with a telemedicine information system, able to improve current medical practice.

The T-IDDM components are described as follows:

- The MU is designed to assists the physician in defining a treatment protocol, that is the assessment of the insulin regimen, diet and physical exercise, through a periodic evaluation of the patient's data. The insulin regimen is specified on the basis of the insulin dosages of regular insulin necessary to compensate for the average meal ingestion, as well as the dosages and timing of nph/lente insulin on the 'typical' day. The MU output is the result of a high-level reasoning process and hence defines a set of prescriptions that is communicated to the PU in order to bound the space of its admissible actions.
- The PU allows for automatic data collection and transmission from the patient's house to the clinic, and assists the patients in their self-monitoring activity, suggesting the insulin dosage adjustments following the control tables contained in the protocol received from the MU. The PU produces an action that is directly performed on the patient, and communicates both the action and the current metabolic state of the patient back to the MU. In this way the MU can follow the actual insulin therapy and the patient's response to it.
- The TIS is devoted to ensure a reliable and efficient communication between the MU and the PU, allowing the two modules to work asynchronously and to exchange data when needed.

The revised previously proposed scenario will hence result as follows: after a periodic visit, the physician will assess a therapeutic protocol, that will be transmitted by the medical unit and received by the patient unit. The patient will be provided with a reflectometer, able to automatically memorize BGL measurement, and will download the measurements in a patient unit, developed on a portable unit or on a PC. The PU will be able to automatically transmit data back to physician, as well as to assist the patient in the self-monitoring activity, providing suggestions and automatic alarms. Moreover, the patient will be able to schedule long-distance consultations or to ask for a new visit. The MU, revising the PU data, will be able to automatically collect data and, through data analysis algorithm, to detect in advance potential dangerous situations, requiring further information from the patient, or suggesting to the physician a protocol revision. In this case, the physician will hence confirm the protocol modification or will require a new visit.

The T-IDDM goal will be hence to provide an effective telemedicine system, whose functionalities will follow the above specified requirements, that have been more deeply investigated in the deliverable D.1.1 (User requirements) of this project. In the following sections the system we propose will be described in detail.

9.3 The telemedicine system overview

The T-IDDM architecture is designed to support a reliable and flexible communication between the system components. The communication system must ensure the required physician-patient interaction through a "PU-MU dialogue", and link the hospital centers to allow exchange of clinical information, statistical data, therapeutic protocols. The components of the communication system must therefore offer, through standard-based facilities, a high-bandwidth and reliable communication path, that should be continuously available and easy to use. In brief, they must be able to:

- Efficiently transmit data between the various components of the architecture;
- Ensure security and authentication of the data;
- Execute reliable checkpointing and backup;
- Efficiently notify emergency situations.

The choice of the network protocol to adopt was guided by the necessity to use standard, low-cost and widely available solutions, so that interoperability with other systems could be easily ensured. The obvious choice was the TCP/IP network protocol, that is the base of the Internet network. Since, for cost reasons, communication between the PU and the MU will take place over public telephone lines, we planned to use the PPP protocol in order to obtain a uniform TCP/IP-based layer.

Above this layer lies the layer of the communication protocol, for which it is possible to resort to the protocols normally used over the Internet: SMTP for electronic mail, FTP for file transfers, HTTP for document distribution in the World-Wide Web environment. The HTTP protocol is the most general, since it subsumes most of the functionalities of the existing client-server protocols. In its simplest form, it allows a client to request a particular piece of information held by the server by specifying its pathname in the server's document space. The protocol provides facilities to perform resource negotiation, authorization checks, etc.

For our purposes, it has been necessary to extend the HTTP protocol from a simple document-retrieval protocol to a protocol through which a client could request an arbitrary service to the server. The resulting protocol, called STSP (Server To Server Protocol), overcomes the strict request-response scheme of HTTP by allowing a bi-directional exchange of information between the client and the server. We have developed an STSP server that allows the user to define new actions that the client can invoke. The STSP protocol will therefore be used to support all forms of communication between the components of the distributed architecture: MU, PU, databases, additional services. It is also used to implement the security services needed when dealing with critical patient data (e.g., cryptography).

On top of this protocol, the actual applications used by patients and physicians are built. Using the services available in the distributed computing environment, they should provide at least the following functionalities:

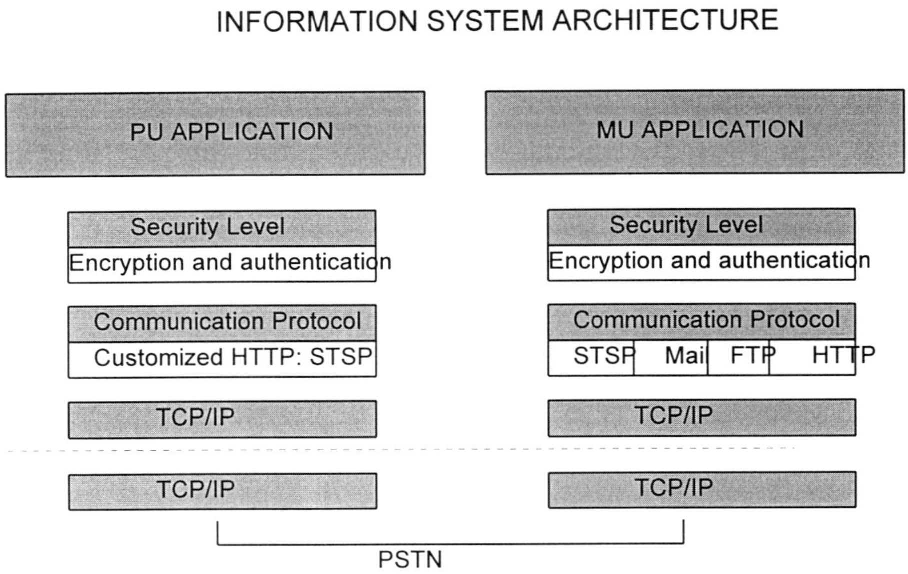

9.4 The Medical Unit Server

The telemedicine service for IDDM patients herein proposed have been realized through a simple hierarchical architecture that relies on the interaction between the MU and the PU. As previously stated, the MU is designed to assist the physician in defining the treatment protocol through the periodic evaluation of patient's data. The treatment protocol is then communicated to the PU in order to bind the space of its admissible actions. The PU assists the patients in their self-monitoring activity, by giving proper therapeutic advice. Moreover, the PU deals with automatic data collection and transmission from the patient's house to the clinic, by communicating the current patient state and therapeutic actions performed. The MU should also guide the PU functionality, by selecting the knowledge sources to be exploited at the patient level: for instance, the PU rules that generate the alarms and suggestions can depend on the patient's life-style. Of course, the two modules may have different computational capabilities. While the PU must perform limited but efficient computations, the MU could resort to more complex techniques in order to properly assist physicians. It is also important to notice that, in a real clinical setting, the two units should usually work asynchronously; in fact, although periodical communications are required, it is not a-priori known when the two modules will be connected. The natural solution to this problem is to develop extended, special-purpose Web servers, that make it possible to create more "intelligent" and "secure" applications while remaining in the context of a Web-based system. For example, one of the most needed features is the ability to communicate with a database. Instead of relying on CGI for this purpose, it is possible to extend the Web server with functions to store values and perform queries, thereby making the database accessible on the WWW in an efficient and straightforward way. An example of this approach is Oracle Web Server, an HTTP server that provides facilities to communicate with a relational database and to generate HTML pages using data extracted from the database. Our approach represents a further step in this direction: we developed a Common Lisp HTTP server, called LispWeb, that allows the web-based application to exploit the full power of a high-level programming language, as well as any number of external services through the network communication facilities that it provides. Applications built using LispWeb have full control over the HTTP transactions that take place between the server and the Web browser, and at the same time can exploit powerful functions to generate HTML pages; moreover, it makes it extremely easy to integrate legacy applications written in Common Lisp, and to make them accessible on the WWW. So, the overall Medical Unit implementation is based on LispWeb.

9.5 The LispWeb development environment

The Medical Unit implements a knowledge-based application composed of the following parts:

- A knowledge base, composed of a structured description of the ontology of the domain under consideration and a long-term data storage
- A reasoning engine, that manipulates the objects contained in the knowledge base;
- A user interface, providing data presentation and knowledge acquisition functionality.

9.5.1 The LispWeb HTTP server

LispWeb is a Common Lisp development environment for distributed applications over the World-Wide Web. It consists of two main modules: an HTTP 1.0 server, and a library of functions to create HTML pages. The HTTP server handles the GET, POST, HEAD, PUT and DELETE methods, performs IP-based and password-based access control, provides request logging and timing, and serves standard HTML pages, images, Java applets and generic binary files. Thanks to its object-oriented nature, it is fully configurable and extensible: for example, users can easily define new methods, specialize the response function for particular classes of requests, or customize the request logging function. The server can be controlled through an HTML interface or by connecting directly to the Lisp interpreter through a Telnet session. The server is also able to act as a TCP client; it can therefore communicate with other servers in a distributed computing environment (databases, mail servers, etc.). The second component of LispWeb is a set of tools to dynamically create HTML pages. Pages are defined using a syntax similar to the one used to define Lisp functions, and are internally represented by the server as Lisp functions; such functions can then be associated with a specific URL, and are run by the server whenever the corresponding URL is requested. The functions, that can take arguments and access global variables defined in the Lisp environment, are responsible for generating the HTML code that will be sent to the client. The developer is provided with a library of HTML-producing Lisp functions, that range from simple tag insertion to high-level formatters able to produce large blocks of HTML code. For example, the LIST-TO-TABLE function takes a list of lists (lists are a primitive data type in Lisp) and produces an HTML table whose rows are the sublists of the input list. Optional arguments can be used to specify additional features of the table, such as border width, cell alignment, and so on. This tool can be extremely powerful, especially in cases where the input list is not known a priori, so that a manual generation of the HTML code would be impossible. Moreover, new functions can be defined to generate frequently-used code fragments (e.g., page banners), thus avoiding unnecessary and time-consuming repetitions on part of the developer. Finally, this approach guarantees that the resulting HTML code will always be syntactically correct and compliant with stylistic recommendations (e.g., all pages must have a TITLE, the HTML, HEAD, and BODY tags are automatically inserted, etc). Other functions allow the values of the header fields, and of the form fields in the case of a POST request, to be examined and possibly modified. This eliminates the need for external GCI scripts, since the same Lisp function can access the field values and generate the appropriate response page. Finally, LispWeb is able to support extensions of the STSP protocol. In particular, we have defined a protocol called STSP, designed to allow a bidirectional exchange of information between two agents. While the HTTP protocol is oriented toward the exchange of request-response messages typical of client-server architectures, the STSP protocol makes it possible to perform more complex forms of negotiation and dialogue between agents. In the following, we will show some examples of the use of this protocol to communicate with external services in a distributed computing environment.

9.5.1.1 The STSP Protocol

STSP is an extension of the HTTP protocol designed to enable a form of communication and cooperation between servers. The HTTP protocol is proving to be a very convenient tool to build distributed hypermedia information systems. It defines a set of services (called methods) that a WWW server is able to offer, and the form of the requests that the clients can perform to the server. Our extension is aimed at supporting more complex interactions between the client and the server, adding features such as bi-directional dialog and resource negotiation, and is realized in a transparent way: it does not modify the way in which the server replies to the usual HTTP methods.

While the usual HTTP methods reference disk files (e.g. GET pathname HTTP/1.0), STSP requests reference tasks and actions. The task structure represents a set of capabilities of the server that refer to a specific domain. The actions define the atomic operations that implement a task; actions are analogous to functions and can take arguments. The structure of an STSP transaction is similar to that of an HTTP request: the client sends a first line containing the requested method (STSP), the task, the action, the action arguments and a protocol specifier, followed by zero or more header lines that specify additional characteristics of the request. The server must reply with a first line containing a protocol identifier and a response code, and with zero or more header lines. After this initial negotiation phase, the client and the server communicate over a bi-directional channel until the invoked action is complete.

9.6 Introduction of security and the T-IDDM requirements

Open networks such as Internet are increasingly being used as a platform for communication in our society. Open and accessible, they allow rapid and efficient world-wide exchanges at low cost. Open networks also have the capacity to offer substantial opportunities for global electronic commerce in goods and services which can be ordered, supplied and paid for electronically.

Nowadays, the advantages provided by the networks can be exploited in the medical field, and in particular in tele-medicine projects. Unfortunately there are some problems related with the architecture of the networks. The most important problem is security. As a matter of fact messages can be intercepted and manipulated, the validity of documents can be denied, personal data can be illicitly collected. For these reasons, it is mandatory to design and realize security solution for the systems connected by open networks In the TIDDM project, therefore, more solutions are worked out to assure more security in data transfer and in data storage, and to assure data integrity and digital signature. The main technique used for obtaining these goals is cryptography.

Two important applications of cryptography are digital signatures and encryption. Digital signatures can help to proving the origin of data (authentication) and verifying whether data has been altered (integrity). Encryption can help keeping data and communication confidential. Because T-IDDM has a client-server architecture, there are several messages sent on the intranet/pstn network that connect the Patient Units and the Medical Unit modules. It is therefore is very important have some mechanism to authenticate the clients and the servers and assure that data is sent on the network in encrypted form.

9.7 An overview of security and cryptography solutions

9.7.1 Cryptographic protocols

Cryptography solves problems that involve security, authentication, integrity, and dishonest people, through the use of different protocols. A cryptographic protocol is a protocol (series of communication steps, involving two or more parties, designed to accomplish a task) that uses cryptography. A cryptographic protocol involves some cryptographic algorithms, but generally the goal of protocol is something beyond simple secrecy. The whole point of using cryptography in a protocol is to prevent or detect eavesdropping and cheating. There are some different protocols which use different cryptographic algorithms, but the most important are:

- Communications using symmetric cryptography;
- One way hash functions;
- Communications using public key cryptography;
- Hybrid cryptosystems;
- Digital Signatures.

9.7.2 Communications using symmetric cryptography

It is easy to suppose that the way for two parties to communicate securely is simply to encrypt their communications, but the complete protocol is more complicated than that. Let us look at what must happen for ‘A’ to send an encrypted message to ‘B’.

- A and B agree on a cryptosystem;
- A and B agree on a key;
- A sends the cipher text message to B;
- B decrypts the ciphertext message with the same algorithm and key.

A good cryptosystem is one in which all the security is inherent in knowledge of the key and none is inherent in knowledge of the algorithm. This is why key management is so important in cryptography. With a symmetric algorithm, A and B can perform step (1) in public, but they must perform step (2) in secret. The key must remain secrete before, during, and after the protocol otherwise the message will no longer be secure. In summary, symmetric cryptosystems have the following problems:

Keys must distributed in secret.

If a key is compromised (stolen, guessed, extorted, etc.), then someone can decrypt all message traffic encrypted with that key. He can also pretend to be one of the parties and produce false message to fool the other party.

Assuming a separate key is used for each pair of users in a network, the total number of keys increases rapidly as the number of users increases. A network of n users requires (n(n-1))/2 keys.

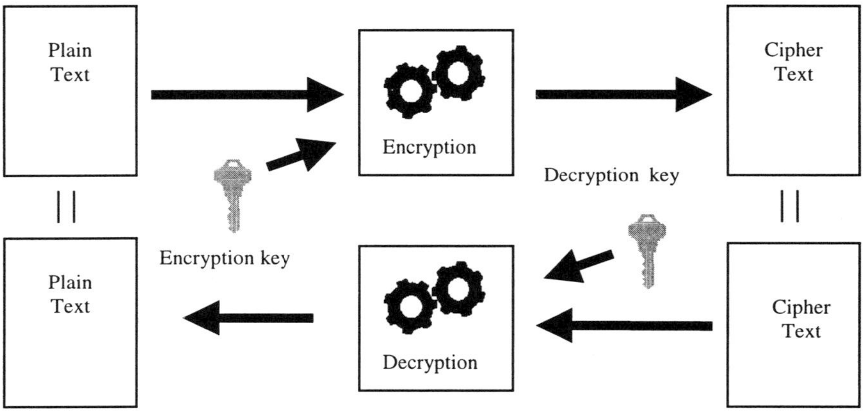

Figure 1: Symmetric cryptosystem.

9.7.3 One-Way Hash Functions

A one way hash function is a function, mathematical or otherwise, that takes a variable-length input string and converts it to a fixed-length output string (called a hash value). A simple hash function would be a function that takes a string and returns a byte consisting of the XOR of all the input bytes. A one-way hash functions is a hash function that works in one direction: It is easy to compute a hash value from input, but it is very hard to generate the input string that hashes to a particular value. The hash function is public, and its security depends on its one-wayness. In the security field, the hash functions can be used to assure data integrity, often using block encryption algorithms.

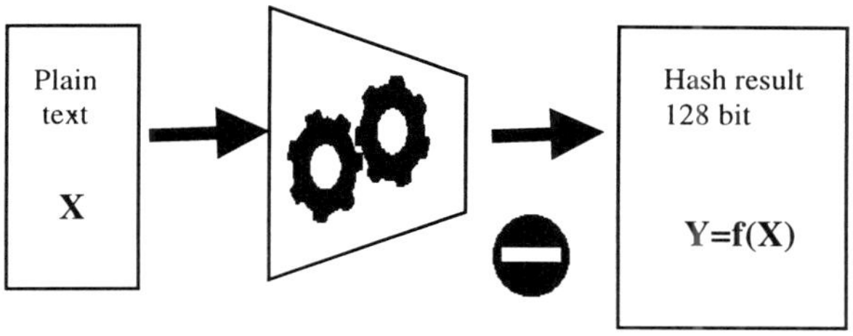

Figure 2: One-way Hash function.

9.7.4 Communications using Public-Key Cryptography

Let us think of a symmetric algorithm as a safe, and the key as its combination. Someone with the combination can open the safe, put document inside, and close it again. Someone else with the combination can open the safe and take the document out. Anyone without the combination is forced to learn safecracking. On the contrary, public-key cryptography used two different keys, one public and the other one private. It is computationally hard to deduce the private key from the public key. Anyone with the public key can encrypt a message but not decrypt it; only the person with the private key can decrypt the message. This is how 'A' can send a message to 'B' using public key cryptography:

- A and B agree on a public-key cryptosystem.
- B sends to A his public-key.
- A encrypts his message using B's public-key and sends it to B.
- B decrypts A's message using his private-key.

Notice how public-key cryptography solves the key-management problem with symmetric cryptosystems. Before A and B had to agree on a key in secret. A could choose one at random, but he still had to get it to B. Public-key cryptography makes this easier, but it still has some problems:

Public-key algorithms are slow. Symmetric algorithms are generally at least 1000 times faster than public-key algorithms.

Public-key cryptosystems are vulnerable to chosen-plaintext attacks. If C=E(P), when P is one plaintext out of set of n possible plaintexts, then a cryptanalyst only has to encrypt all n possible plaintexts and compare the result with C. He won't be able to recover the decryption key this way, but he will be able to determine P.

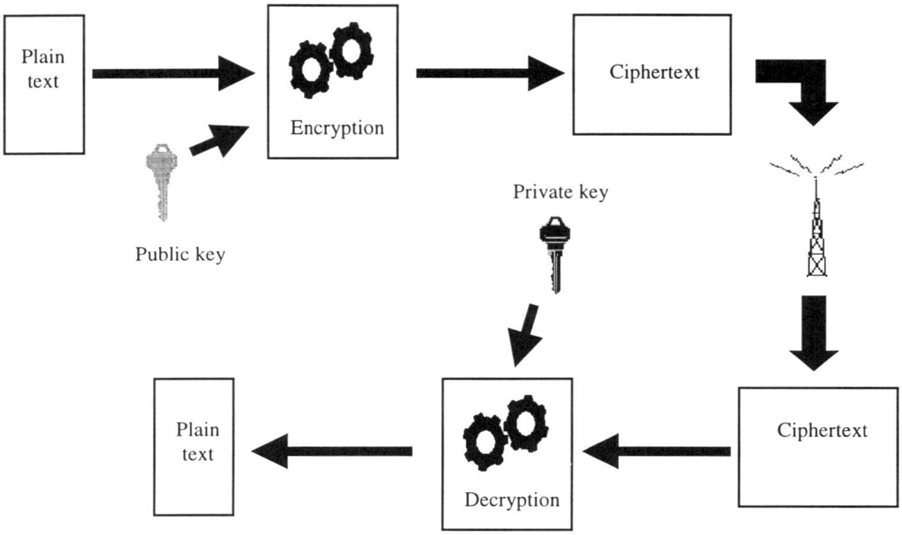

Figure 3: Public-key cryptosystem.

For these reasons in the most practical implementation public-key cryptography is used with symmetric cryptography in the Hybrid Cryptosystem.

9.7.5 Hybrid Cryptosystem

In this protocol the public-key cryptography is used to secure and to distribute session keys: those session keys are used with symmetric algorithms to secure message traffic. The steps in this protocol are:

- B sends A his public-key;
- A generates a random session key, K, encrypts it using B's public-key, and sends it to B as E(K);
- B decrypts A's message using his private-key to recover the session-key. D(E(K))=K
- Both of them encrypt their communications using the same session key.

Using public-key cryptography for key distribution solves a very important key management problem. With symmetric cryptography, the data encryption key sits around until is used. With the previous protocol, the session key is created when it is needed to encrypt communications and destroyed when it is no longer needed. This drastically reduces the risk of compromising the session key. Of course, the private-key is vulnerable to compromise, but it is only used once per communication to encrypt a session key and it is possible change it always.

9.7.6 Digital signatures

In practical implementation, public-key algorithms are often too inefficient to sign long documents. To save time, digital signature protocols are often implemented with one-way hash functions. Instead of signing a document, A signs the hash of the document. In this protocol, both the one-way hash function and the digital signature algorithm are used. The main steps are:

- A produces a one-way hash of a document.
- A encrypts the hash with his private-key, thereby signing the document.
- A sends both the document and the signed hash to B.
- B produces a one-way hash of the document that A sent. He then, using the digital signature algorithm, decrypts the signed hash with A's public-key. If the signed hash matches the hash he generated, the signature is valid.

Speed increased drastically and, since the chances of two different documents having the same 160-bit hash are only one in 2^{160} anyone can safely equate a signature of the hash with a signature of the document.

9.8 TIDDM implementation

After having identified the various solutions presented in the literature, these steps were followed:

- Use the Hybrid protocol with a few alterations to fit it to the TIDDM's STSP protocol.
- Use RSA as the public key algorithm.
- Use IDEA as the symmetric algorithm.
- Use MD5 as a hash function.
- Develop some functions in C language to implement this protocol in the TIDDM system.

9.8.1 Secure STSP

Secure STSP is the extension of the STSP protocol that develops a Hybrid protocol for the TIDDM system.

In this protocol the public-key algorithm (RSA) is used to crypt the session key (in this case, the client's password). In every session the server generates a new pair of keys (public and private) and the client must keep the public-key and crypt its credentials.

After the response by the Server, that checks whether the client is authorized, the client and the server can exchange the data. The data are encrypted by a symmetric algorithm (IDEA). Steps are illustrated in Figure 4.

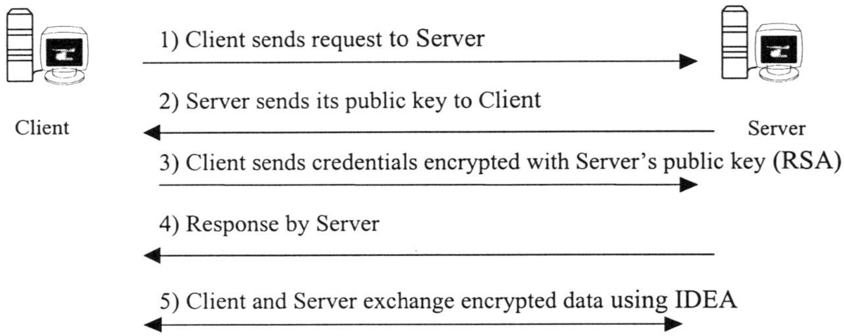

Figure 4: Steps for Secure STSP protocol.

9.8.2 Secure STSP implementation

We developed a library in C language implementing servers and clients that support Secure-STSP-protocol.

The functions in the library allow to use authentication procedures and to send and receive ciphertext. For making the Server there are four functions that initialize and start the server. These functions are:

*void new_task(char *task_name).*
*void new_action(char *task_name,char *action_name,int secure).*
*void add_function(char *task_name,char *action_name, HANDLER function).*
void Server(int port).

The *new_task* function defines a new task in the server (see STSP protocol).
The *new_action* function defines the action for tasks defined before and its security level, if the value of *secure* parameter is *0* then the protocol chosen is standard STSP, while if it is *1* then the protocol is Secure-STSP. The *add_function* defines which function the server must call when the particular request (task, action) is received. To create a server, the user must write and compile in object form its functions, and write a configuration file that include all server's specifications. The mechanisms and the file format are illustrated in Figure 5. In this way the authentication process is automatic when the user sets to *1* the secure parameter. The Server function starts the server on the port specified. Therefore there are some functions to initialize and transmit with the IDEA algorithm.

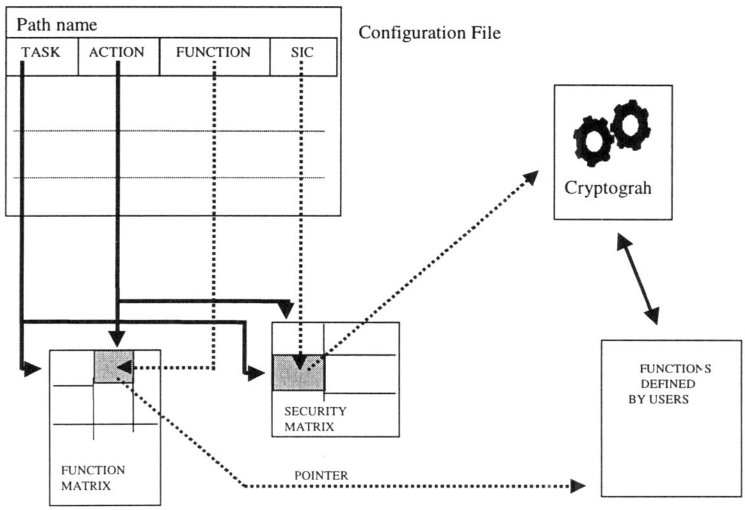

Figure 5: STSP library mechanism.

These functions are divided into two groups, for the servers and for the clients. The servers' functions are:

*InitSender(char *key).*
*SenderSend(char *message).*
CloseSender().

The *InitSender* allows to set the key to crypt the data and initialize data structures. The IDEA algorithm is modified to crypt the data not in the whole but row by row, as their are sent. To encrypt and send all data in fact we must call *SenderSend* repeatedly, and when the data is finished we must call *CloseSender* to dispose of the data structures and close the stream. On the other hand the functions receiving the ciphertext are:

*InitReceiver(char *key).*
*ReceiverGet(char *message).*
CloseReceiver().

The *InitReceiver* function is like *InitSender*: it allows to set the key to decrypt the data and initialize data structures. For receiving and decrypting ciphertext from the net we must use *ReceiveGet* many times until it returns a particular value that represents the end of read data. Finally to dispose of data structures and to close the stream we have to call *CloseReceiver*. At the end, to calculate the data's digital signatures there is a function that implements the MD5 algorithm.

*MD5hash(char *data).*

With this function it is possible to calculate the data hash value; this can be sent together with the ciphertext to check data integrity.

9.9 Conclusions

This project is primarily concerned with a specific therapy, but has become involved in the security area as a result of the revised scenario for this therapy. The project set out to provide an effective telemedicine service for the revised scenario. This means supporting reliable and flexible communications between the system components throughout the therapy cycle. Such system components connected through open networks must have security solutions for data integrity and authentication as a prerequisite for effective operation. The project has looked to known protocols and cryptography solutions for support and in general this has provided the sort of infrastructure that was needed, although in some cases the protocols have had to be extended and the project has become involved in detailed technical work in this area.

Looking to the future, the experience gained in this project and other projects has now to be built on in order to ensure that "security infrastructure" becomes just another system component to be incorporated into these important "telemedicine" applications. One of the goals is to be able to remove the "telemedicine" descriptor as an element of added complication, so that these sort of projects will be able to concentrate on processes to deliver patient and clinical value.

For more information on T-IDDM please contact:

Riccardo Bellazzi, PhD
E-mail: ric@ipvaimed3.unipv.it

Case Studies of Security Problems and their Solutions
G.O. Klein (Ed.)
IOS Press, 2000

10. Security Aspects in Relation to the HISA Standard Middleware Architecture

Fabrizio Ferrara

10.1 Abstract

The integration and evolution of existing systems represents one of the most urgent priorities of health care information systems in order to allow the whole organisation to meet the increasing clinical organisational and managerial needs. The ENV 12967-1 'Healthcare Information Systems Architecture' standard defines an architectural approach based on a middleware of business-specific common services, enabling all parts of the local and geographical system to rely on a common information heritage of patient, clinical, administrative and managerial data.

Thanks to the availability of industrial products conforming to the standard, the effectiveness and the validity of this approach is now extensively used in the production and commercial environment. Industrial collaborations have been also established, based on the development and distribution of integratable and complementary components of a common, open healthcare-information system, based on the common DHE middleware.

After an overview on the key aspects of the HISA architecture, this paper discusses the positioning of the authorisation and security aspects in the overall architectural framework and presents the specific features implemented in the industrial DHE middleware.

10.2 The Middleware-based architectural approach

10.2.1 The evolution needs of Health care Information Systems

By nature, health care organisational structure is distributed, being a geographical spread of centres at different levels of complexity: from the general hospitals down to individual GPs. Also the structure of the individual health care centre, and particularly of the hospitals, is evolving from a vertical, aggregated organisation, towards the integration of a set of specialised departments, which are characterised by diverse logistic, organisational and clinical requirements and aspects. The ultimate objective of such a structure is to build a network of complementary centres (hospitals, laboratories, ambulatories, co-ordination centres, etc.) spread over the territory, individually autonomous but also capable of interworking to meet effectively the health and social needs in the area, and to provide seamless care.

From the information technology point of view, such overall scenario is presently characterised by a huge number of different, heterogeneous and mutually incompatible applications, which are already installed and operational in the individual centres, to support specific needs of particular groups of users.

Both at local and territorial level, therefore, the objective is to allow the evolution, integration and the consistent interworking of different (heterogeneous) applications, even if they have been developed in different moments, by different vendors and with different technologies.

The technological connection of distributed systems (as allowed through generic middlewares and components like COM and Corba) is necessary and useful, but does not provide any contribution to the real inter-operability and inter-working of the systems from the point of view of application-oriented support to user needs. Also the simple exchanging of messages is not enough, since it can only allow a certain, loosely coupled, interworking among different sectors, without really gluing the health care organisation as a whole.

As it occurs for any other business scenarios, also the overall healthcare organisation can be considered as a set of users, individually different and doing specific jobs, but all needing to rely and to share a set of common fundamental data, as shown in Figure 1.

Such common data may not be under the ownership of individual applications and/or suppliers, but must be accessible to all (present and future) applications through public and stable interfaces, which should also not depend on any specific technical characteristic and/or system configuration.

Without the need of going back to centralised, monolithic information systems, such goal may be obtained by organising the health care information system according to a comprehensive, open and standard architecture. All of that, by securing the investments already made, permitting the continuity of the service and facilitating a gradual evolution of the existing legacy systems towards new approach.

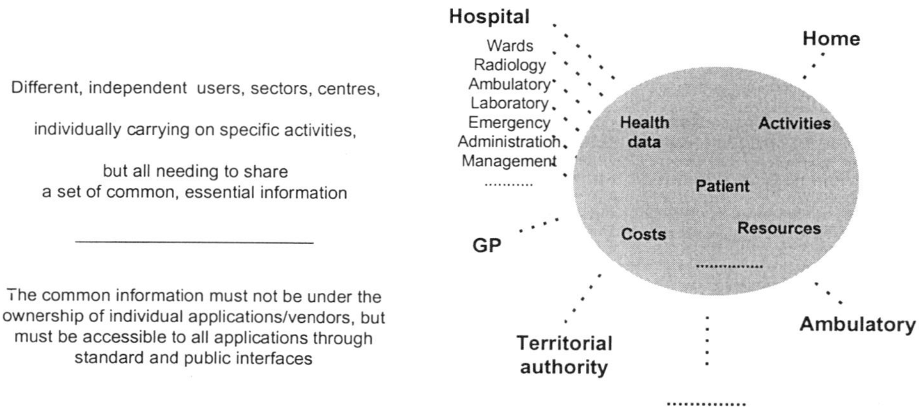

Figure 1: The fundamental rationale of the open architecture.

10.2.2 The structure of the standard architecture

As it is defined in the CEN/TC251 ENV 12967-1 standard 'Health care Information Systems Architecture', the objectives and requirements discussed in the previous paragraphs may be effectively satisfied and supported by structuring the architecture of the information system through three co-operative layers, individually responsible for addressing specific needs of the organisation, as shown in Figure 2:

APPLICATIONS	consisting of a set of components responsible for interacting with the users, providing a specialised support to the various activities carried out in the various sectors of the health care organisation.
MIDDLEWARE	providing a set of services which support the whole system with respect to the management of those common data and procedures of paramount relevance for the whole organisation.
BITWAYS	representing the technological platform, providing facilities enabling the various modules of the information system to interact through common mechanisms, hiding the diverse technologies adopted for their implementation and the mutual location over the (distributed) environment.

With respect to the middleware, the HISA standard identifies the following six fundamental groups of services (HCS: Health care Common Services):

Subject of Care HCS	responsible for providing services for defining and managing personal, administrative and epidemiological data on the patients and other subjects of care, with their cases and contacts
Activity HCS	responsible for providing services for defining and managing the life-cycle of the activities performed in the organisation, from the initial request, to the planning, execution and reporting.
Health characteristics HCS	responsible for providing services for defining and managing health data and characteristics of the subjects of care.
Resource HCS	responsible for providing services for defining and managing the resources of the organisation
Authorisation HCS	responsible for providing services for defining and managing the specification of the users allowed to operate with the system and their authorisations with respect to the execution of the various processes and access to the data
Concepts HCS	responsible for providing services for defining and managing rules and properties involving multiple types of data.

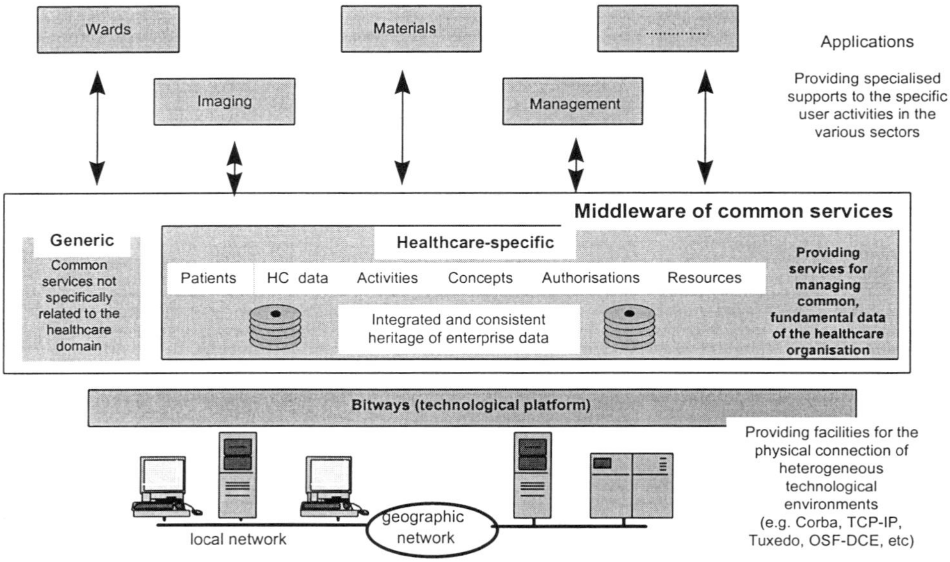

Figure 2: The 3-layers structure of the CEN architecture of health care information systems (applications just represent examples).

10.2.3 Strategic benefits deriving from the middleware

The presence of the middleware satisfies the needs above, thus:

- the functional and information consistency of the overall organisation is ensured through the presence of the middleware, which is actually responsible for dealing with those activities and information which exceed the level of responsibility of the individual units (or complete centres);
- the individual characteristics of the individual units may be satisfied by leaving users free to select the most appropriate applications capable of supporting their needs, and just requesting that such applications are federated on top of the middleware through its public, standard API's;
- the existing legacy systems may continue to be used and may be federated on top of the middleware, by invoking its services through the relevant (public, standard) API.

The essence of the HISA standard is that **information represent a common heritage and must be clearly separated from the applications**, to be available where and when needed to the various modules of the information system.

Through its services for the definition and management of the information common to the whole organisation, the middleware represents both the key element for ensuring the openness and modularity of the information system, and an operational infrastructure suitable for the integration of legacy systems and for the development of new modules.

Since applications do not interact directly with the data storage(s) (e.g. the DBMS), but access and manipulate the data through the services of the middleware, the physical configuration of the overall information system can be optimised and evolved during the time without the need of introducing modifications in the applications. As a consequence, even different products (e.g. DBMS) can coexist, distributed environment can be (gradually) implemented and evolved, and even existing legacy modules of the information system — once encapsulated with proper services — can be used as components of the middleware, accessible from all other applications.

Finally, new applications can be developed without the need of designing and implementing ad-hoc (and fragmented) databases, but directly using the services of the middleware for accessing and manipulating the totality of the relevant data, both those directly generated by them and those created by other applications of the system.

This approach not only ensures the automatic integration of the new application in the overall system, but also permits to dramatically reduce the development and maintenance times and costs. With this respect, it is worthwhile to consider that — in any generic project — only one third of the total development time is — in average — devoted for the implementation of those functionalities supporting specific business activities of the addressed sector. More than two thirds of the total development time are spent for the implementation of those basic but fundamental functionalities necessary for the definition and management (i.e. enter, modify, delete) of the data. Through the adoption of a middleware, this cost can be dramatically reduced, by reducing it to the sole development of marginal extensions in the middleware, to permit the management of those data that are not already supported.

Figure 3 shows the complete scenario, integrating both legacy systems and new applications, allowing — in parallel — the achieving of the following benefits for the organisation:

- the existing applications continue working as before, relying on their own data and functionalities;
- the common information structure of the organisation, suitable to support also the need of new applications, is created and automatically fed by the existing applications during the daily activities;
- the evolution may be carried out stepwise, by implementing also partial integrations[32] between different sectors/applications, to provide quick and effective answers to specific business needs.

The HISA middleware services also represent a suitable mechanism for supporting **healthcare record** systems. In fact, according also to what defined in the CEN ENV 12665 'Electronic Healthcare Record Architecture', the healthcare record is an aggregation of information which '*may contain anything*'. Each user must be free to include the various types of information in the healthcare record of one patient, according to the specific needs, depending on reasons based e.g. on the clinical speciality, the health conditions of the patient, the organisational needs, etc. On the other side, information being included in the healthcare record is not usually generated 'per-se', but is the result of some activities

---

[32] I.e. relating to only a part of the data managed by the applications.

carried out with respect to the patient, and may also represent fundamental data to support a number of other processes in the organisation. E.g. the same information on a request for radiology examination (being part of the HCR of the patient) are also necessary for planning purpose in the radiology department, for accounting reasons in the administrative department and from the clinical point of view to the physicians/technicians actually performing the examination.

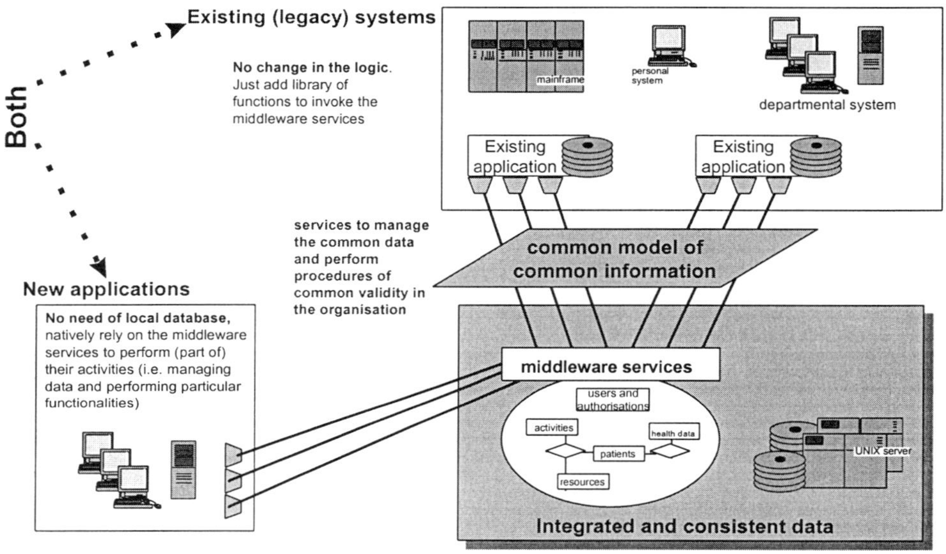

Figure 3: The complete scenario, integrating both legacy systems and applications on top of the middleware.

On the basis of such requirements, from the engineering point of view, the HCR can be considered as an aggregation of (parts of) the whole information available in the information system, being clustered according to different views, criteria and perspectives according to the specific needs and characteristics of the individual users.

As a consequence, healthcare record systems may refer to the common data of the organisation through the services of the HISA middleware, by manipulating and presenting the information according to the needs of the specific users, nevertheless preserving the integration and consistency of the information heritage. Moreover, the consistency of the HISA specification with the EHCRA standard, also simplifies the engineering structure of the HCR /EPR systems, which can directly rely on the middleware services, without the need of implementing local data stores.

10.3 Key-facts on the DHE implementation of the CEN standard

The DHE® (Distributed Healthcare Environment) represents a middleware conformant to the HISA Standard, implementing a (distributed) repository for all clinical, organisational and managerial information of the healthcare structure, to make them available when and where necessary to all applications in the healthcare information system.

Information stored in the DHE may be entered, modified and retrieved through a set of services, which are accessible to the applications by means of stable and **public** API's, not depending on any physical or technological environment. Such API's are provided through libraries (i.e. DLL in Windows environment), accessible by the applications.

Information and functional aspects

The information of the healthcare organisation is efficiently organised in an integrated structure over centralised or distributed configuration, capable to support both the daily production requirements and statistical, data-warehousing analyses. The DHE natively supports the fundamental set of information concepts managed by any type of healthcare organisation, including:

- personal, epidemiological and statistic data on patients, contacts and cases;
- clinical and organisational activities activities (from complete protocols and treatments, up to elementary tasks) during the whole life-cycle: from initial requesting up to booking, planning, executing, reporting, etc.
- structure of the organisation, from the territorial aspects, up to the centres, units and individual agents;
- resources (drugs, staff, materials, equipment, locations) available and actually used, also in relationship with the activities performed;
- patients health data, also as outcomes of the activities, individually and with the view of the patient healthcare record;
- diagnostic, administrative and clinical classifications;
- managerial data including the budgeted and actual utilisation of resources, costs, performance indicators, for the various sectors of the organisation, also in relationship with the patients cared and activities performed.

Specific services employ more complex functionalities (such as the requesting, booking, planning and reporting of activities).

Technical issues

Through the DHE a real multi-tier, open and scalable client/server architecture (conforming to Levels 3 and 4 of Gartners-Group classification) is automatically implemented, allowing Unix, Windows and Mac applications to be connected with the DHE, always ensuring optimal performances, suitable for on-line interactive processing.

The technological environments currently supported ensure a full range of scalability, starting from single Windows NT systems and evolving — without any change in the application — up to distributed multi-server environments, integrating Windows and Unix systems (including Sun, HP, DEC, IBM, etc.), interacting through both local networks and Internet.

Replication of transactions and of data across a distributed environment is managed by the DHE in a modality completely transparent to the application, according to criteria which can be in each individual configuration by the local technical responsibles.

The preferred DBMS's (including Oracle, Sybase, Informix and Microsoft SQL-Server) are supported, interacted by the DHE through their native interfaces to ensure the most effective performances. Even different DBMS's may coexist in the same environment. Detailed logging and statistical analyses are also provided for auditing, tuning and legal purposes.

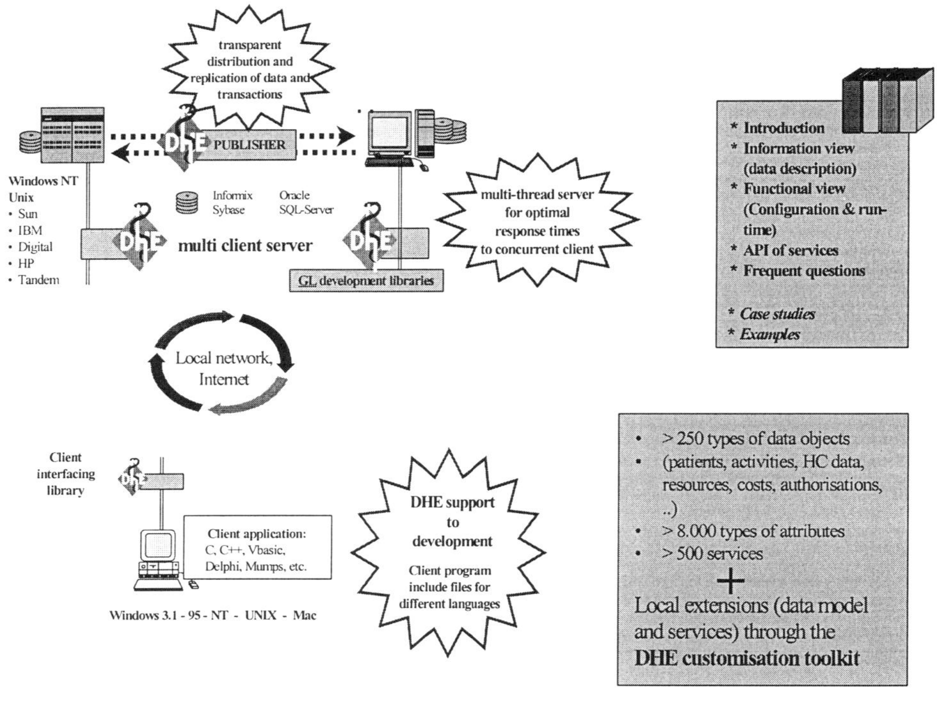

Figure 4: The DHE technical environment.

Extensions and customisations

The over 250 data objects and 8.000 data attributes already pre-defined in the DHE already ensure the support to the almost totality of the usual requirement of any healthcare information system. Nevertheless, should additional information and/or functional requirements be identified in one specific environment, the native data model and services of the DHE middleware can be extended by the users according to their specific local needs, even autonomously without the need of depending on external suppliers.

To facilitate this task, the DHE toolkit -running on any stand-alone or networked MS-Windows PC- provides a set of CASE and run-time functionalities, which allow to extend the common information and functional model with the specification of additional data elements, and of additional services. The DHE toolkit also supports the whole software production life cycle, from the verification of the integrity of the specification, up to the generation of the software code (in C and SQL language) for the extensions.

10.4 Authorisation and security in the middleware-based architecture

10.4.1 Authorisation and security

The term 'security' is frequently used to generically refer to all aspects relating to the identification and authorisation and validation of one agent (either individual or software process) in the information system.

Many organisation, technological and operational requirements and implications are related to such concepts. Approaching them all together in one unique term (or component of the information system) is extremely complex and risky with respect to the final results.

An incremental methodological approach — as recommended by the ODP and HISA — based on different levels of abstraction and on different perspectives may be beneficial for simplify the whole matter.

By proceeding top-down from the user (organisational) point of view towards the more technological and implementation-oriented aspects, it is therefore possible to analyse the whole problem from different perspectives, by identifying smaller, self-consistent issues, complementary each-other, but individually more easily formalisable and manageable.

We can first of all identify a set of requirements related to how the healthcare organisation is structured and on how the individual users carry on their daily activities. Such aspects formalise the rules according to which each (type of) user is authorised to perform certain tasks (e.g. registering a diagnosis), as well as to access/manipulate certain data, both clinical and administrative (e.g. the results of some tests of one patient, the salary of other employees, etc.).

It is important to stress that such issues are completely independent from any technological and implementation aspect of the system. They just relate to the organisation and to the laws and procedures, which are in force in that place or country. As a consequence, they may largely vary across countries, regions and even individual centres of the same city.

On the other side, however, it can be noted that the identification of a clear and common set of terms of reference on how to formalise and manage such aspects represents a fundamental pre-requisite for any implementation initiative. Without that, the information system would not be able to effectively support how the organisation operates.

This set of requirements and the formalisation of a comprehensive, technological independent, framework for their description and management can be more properly referred to with the term '**<u>Authorisation</u>**'.

Through this term, therefore, we will refer to:

a) the organisational task aiming at defining the rules according to which each user is allowed to perform certain tasks and to access certain data

b) the conceptual model of such rules, in a way suitable for taking into account the diversity of the individual organisation and through notations and criteria independent on specific technological implementations

c) the part of the actual information system responsible for implementing that model and for storing the actual (local) rules in a comprehensive and consistent modality, making them available to the various applications

A **different** (but complementary) set of aspects, relates to the mechanisms, tools, and technologies according to which the authorisation part of the information system (as well as the other parts) are implemented in practice, with a view of supporting those organisational requirements related to the secure authentication of the agents (i.e. individuals and software processes) performing the various tasks, to the reliable communication of information between two agents, to the archiving of information according to legal and ethical requirements. This set of aspects will be referred to with the term '**Security**'.

In the three-layer model of the HISA architecture, different classes of services (and of components) are responsible for the Authorisation and for the Security aspects.

The formalisation of the model and the management of the information related to the authorisation rules and criteria are under the responsibility of the healthcare-specific services of the middleware. The mechanisms, tools and technologies according to which the security requirements are implemented are under the responsibility of the 'bitways' layer of the architecture. Obviously, generic services are employed by the middleware and by the applications to operate according to the security requirements imposed in the specific organisation.

It may be stressed that a generic model and a common set of services may be identified for the management of the authorisation aspects throughout all information systems. On the other side, due to the diversities in the rules, budget, cultural characteristics of the various organisations, it is very difficult to envisage a unique, standard set of security technologies being implemented in all healthcare information systems of all European countries. Moreover, the fast moving of the research and of the market in this field rapidly makes obsolete the various products. An open environment, therefore, should conform to the following fundamental rules:

a) To provide a common framework and a common set of services for allowing all applications and components to retrieve the authorisation aspects of the organisation and to operate accordingly;

b) To foresee a set of 'sockets' in the physical implementation, allowing to simply plug-in additional components and services responsible for providing specific security features (in case none, should they not be requested in the organisation)

In the following section 10.4.2, the authorisation aspects of the HISA standard and of the DHE middleware will be discussed.

Section 10.4.3 will then describe the security facilities currently implemented in the DHE middleware. With this respect, it must be emphasised how the open physical architecture of the DHE allows a high degree of modularity also to such features, allowing to substitute them with other products and even to completely remove them, should the characteristics of the organisation require to do so.

10.4.2 Authorisation aspects in HISA and in the DHE

As it has been presented in Section 10.2, the HISA standard prescribes a set of services (i.e. Authorisation HCS) to be present in the middleware for allowing the applications and the other components to define and manage the specification of the users allowed to operate with the system and their authorisations with respect to the execution of the various processes and access to the data

With this respect, it has to be considered that, besides the need for supporting the diversification of roles and responsibilities which is typical of any type of large organisation, additional critical aspects can be identified in the healthcare scenario due to the particular type of information which is managed, implying also ethical and legal aspects.

Moreover, different responsibilities can be identified in the healthcare organisation regarding the role and activities of the users. Moving from country to country or from one healthcare centre to another, different types or levels of authorisation may be applied to similar types of users, both for execution of particular functions and for access to the information.

The Authorisation Common Services in the middleware layer of HISA aim at supporting this specific need, by providing:

- a comprehensive and consistent repository where those responsible in the organisation may define the rules according to which the different users may execute the functions provided by the system;
- a standard mechanism in terms of services available and information managed, according to which the rest of the system may check whether one user is allowed to perform the activities they are requesting.

It is stressed again that the functionalities provided by these Common Services are completely independent of any kind of complementary security mechanism that may be defined and implemented in the system to secure and protect the individual data.

The rationale underlying the data model foreseen by HISA for this set of middleware services, is based on the understanding that the entire HIS consists of a number of components, being either applications or common services. From its internal perspective, each component interacts with various external agents, which may be either individual users or other components.

Each component may be described in terms of a set of controlled functionalities, whose invocation and manipulation by external agents is subject to specific authorisations.

For each component, a set of authorisation profiles are defined, usually reflecting the various jobs and responsibilities in the organisational area where the system is operating. Each authorisation profile may operate with a set of controlled functionalities,

according to one set of conditions, which describe its authorisation in terms of a set of information, such as:
- working ways which define whether the profile is allowed to access that element by adding new data or reading, updating, or deleting existing data;
- time frame which permits the specification of the temporal limits of the authorisation, through a start and end time every day;
- days of the week which specify the individual days of the week when the agent is allowed to interact with the object;
- workstations, which specify a list of workstations or nodes of the information system from which the agent is allowed to interact with the object.

Subject to specific individual approval, defined in the specific conditions, any generic agent of one profile may be authorised to define agents of the same profile as well as of other profiles of the system.

Each agent of the HIS can be characterised by a name, a unique public identifier, e.g. a code, and some mechanisms for ensuring its correct identification. To access a component, the agent must be a member of one authorisation profile of that component. Such membership is granted by another individual agent, and is valid in a specific time period only, i.e. between a starting and an expiration date.

Exceptions may be also defined, in terms of extensions or limitations of the authorisation of one individual agent, with respect to the standard authorisations defined for its profile. Also such exceptions must be defined by one individual agent and are described through a set of conditions

On the basis of this rationale, data being maintained through these services is schematised in Figure 5. By referring to what stated in the HISA document, the following considerations may be pointed out with respect to the identified classes of data.

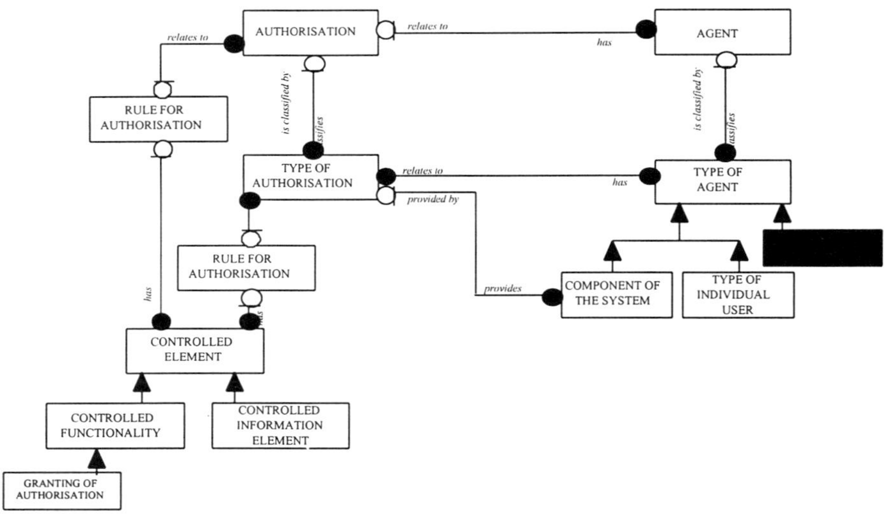

Figure 5: The Data model of the middleware Authorisation Common services.

An **Agent** is an individual user or a software component authorised to interact with the information system. Each agent is classified through a 'type of agent', which allows the organisation to identify the fundamental groups (e.g. on the basis of the job-description). It is worth emphasising how one (set of) type of agents related to the software components of the information systems. In increasingly distributed systems, in fact, the regulation of and the protection from external automated interactions represents a major concern.

On the other side, the entity 'Controlled elements' provides the classification of the elements of the system — e.g. data elements, functionalities, devices — for which authorisation mechanisms are defined by the healthcare organisation.

The general procedures according to which the types of agents may access and operate with the controlled elements may be formalised through the 'Type of Authorisation' and the relevant 'Rules for Authorisation'.

Each agent inherits the authorisations defined for his/her class (i.e. type of agent). Should (as it frequently happens) some particular cases occur (e.g. vacancy, temporary substitution, etc.) individual authorisations overriding the generic values may be formalised.

This model is very flexible and allows describing the widest set of requirements and rules, easily supporting therefore any type of healthcare organisation.

It is worth to stress that it represents a suitable framework also for the formalisation of the specific **Security** mechanisms, which have to be adopted in the individual cases. E.g. the authorisation rules specified in the middleware for a certain class of agents may also comprise the specification of the particular encryption / signature criteria to be adopted when authenticating one agent.

The DHE middleware fully implements such model and provides the services enabling the other (local and remote) components of the information system to retrieve information on the specific authorisations applicable for the various agents when accessing the various controlled elements (i.e. executing tasks and/or accessing data).

In addition to that, the DHE also implements authorisation information at the level of each instance stored in the database, allowing a more direct and focused verification of the ownership and accessibility of each individual elementary datum.

For such a purpose an 'ownership stamp' is managed for each record, specifying the level of accessibility of that record: i.e.

- restricted to the initial creator,
- accessible (read only or modifiable) by other agents in the same organisational unit (e.g. the other physicians of the ward)
- accessible (read only or modifiable) by other agents outside the organisational unit (e.g. physicians outside the hospital)

10.4.3 Security features in the DHE

In the physical implementation of the DHE, several security features are also implemented, as it is briefly schematised in the following. It is emphasised again how the open architecture of the middleware makes it possible to substitute and even to remove such features in the individual installations, according to the specific local regulations, laws and needs.

As a consequence, also evolutions in the related technologies and results of new research initiatives may be easily integrated by the locally responsible and by third parties in the common framework.

Encrypted communications

Encryption/decryption modules based on private and public keys may be activated on both the client and the server side, to allow secure communications between the different components over the network (i.e. both client-server and server to server).

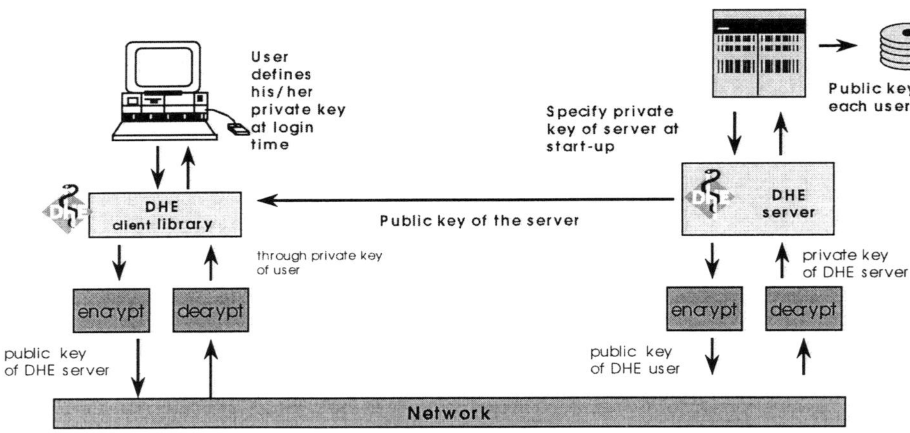

Figure 6: Secure communications implemented by the middleware.

Digital signature

The user may add a digital signature when validating and entering health data into the system (e.g. diagnosis, results of tests, and even images). The digital signature is calculated by the DHE on the basis of the contents of the data being signed and on the key of the validating user. A verification function allows validating the authenticity of the signed data, by analysing the digital signature with respect to the actual data. This approach allows a significant reduction of the system overhead as well as of the needed disk capacity and of the network traffic, nevertheless ensuring the validity of the data (in conformance with most regulations in force in several European countries).

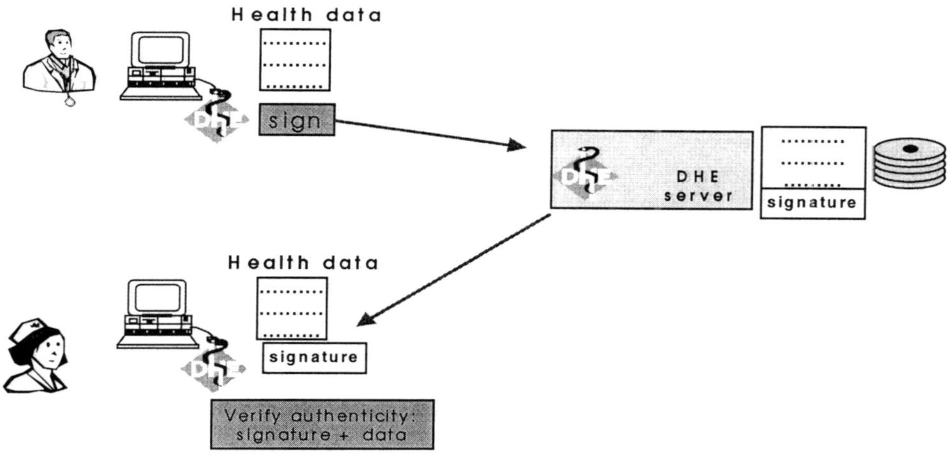

Figure 7: The digital signature for health data.

Certification of the user activities

In some cases, for auditing and/or legal purposes it may be useful to keep a detailed log of all activities carried out by the individual users, with the sequence of the data accessed and manipulated. To ensure the privacy and the legal validity of such information (to be accessible to the sole involved users and/or authorised delegates), the DHE provides a 'log & encrypt' feature, as shown in the following figure. The DHE generates a log of all interactions occurred with one user; the generated file is then signed and encrypted by the user by using his/her private keys. By both ensuring the privacy of the registered information and impeding any modification in the log, such mechanisms makes also the DHE compliant with some legal requirements being introduced in some European countries (e.g. Italian law N. 59 of April 1997).

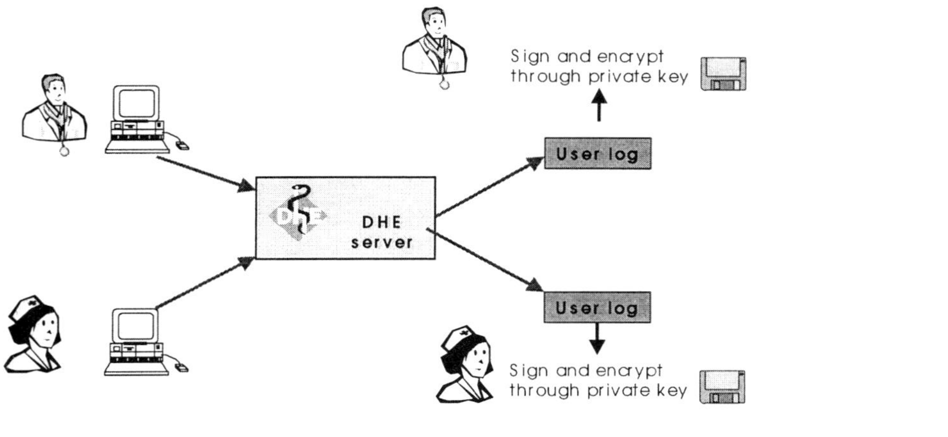

Figure 8: The certification of the activities of the individual users.
Figure 8: The certification of the activities of the individual users.

10.5 Conclusions

Through its services for the definition and management of the information common to the whole organisation, the middleware represents both the key element for ensuring the openness and modularity of the information system, and an operational infrastructure suitable for the integration of legacy systems and for the development of new modules.

The rationale underlying the data model foreseen by HISA is based on the understanding that the entire HIS consists of a number of components, being either applications or common services. From its internal perspective, each component interacts with various external agents, which may be either individual users or other components.

Each component may be described in terms of a set of controlled functionalities, whose invocation and manipulation by external agents is subject to specific authorisations.

For each component, a set of authorisation profiles are defined, usually reflecting the various jobs and responsibilities in the organisational area where the system is operating.

References

CEN/TC251 ENV 12967-1 'Health care Information Systems Architecture'.

CEN/TC251 ENV12265 'Electronic Health care Record Architecture'.

The DHE middleware: — Information view, Functional view and API's — SPRI 1998.

A. Bakker, et al. International Journal of Medical Informatics, Special Issue Common Security problems for communicating patient data. Vol.49, No. 1, March 1998.

H.L. Bleich, W.V. Slack 'Design of a hospital information system: a comparison between integrated and interfaced systems', MedInfo 92.

G. Buonomo: Italian Laws and regulations concerning the creation, storage and transmission of documents by means of computer-based systems and digital signatures. OECD-EMEF Workshop on Cryptography Policy, Paris Dec. 1997.

F.M. Ferrara, 'The management of authorisations and security in health care information systems', in 'Towards security in medical telematics', IOS Press, 1995.

European Commission: Proposal for a European Parliament and Council Directive on a common framework for electronic signatures COM (1998) 297 final, Brussels, 13 May 1998.

Gazzetta Ufficiale delle Repubblica Italiana. Legge 59/1997.

G. Klein et al. "Trusted Health Information Systems", SPRI, Infosec-94 programme, Stockholm 1994.

S. Sphani, J.R. Scherrer, D. Sauquet, P.A. Sottile. 'Consensual trends for optimising the constitution of middleware', SYNAPSES project, Telematics Application Programme of the Commission of the European Communities, project No. HC1046.

For more information:
Fabrizio Massimo Ferrara
E-mail: fmf@gesi.it

Case Studies of Security Problems and their Solutions
G.O. Klein (Ed.)
IOS Press, 2000

11. Using S/MIME for Health Insurance Claims

Tim Benson

11.1 Abstract

This chapter describes a specific case study which was looking at an alternative approach using a commercially available mail client software to securely transfer health insurance claims from UK doctors to private health insurers. The chapter outlines the background to the search for an alternative approach, the methods used, some summary feedback from the experience and some conclusions to be drawn. This chapter highlights the importance of sharing experiences on as wide a scale as possible both within health and without in such a complex field.

11.2 Background to the Healthcare Insurance Claims Submission project

The submission and payment of healthcare insurance claims is an important electronic commerce application. Security is vital, because claims contain sensitive identifiable patient information. This case study describes the implementation of S/MIME on stand-alone PCs connected to the Internet. It shows that implementing "standard" tools is not quite as simple as the advertisements may suggest.

In the UK some 14,000 doctors submit claims for private healthcare treatment to the healthcare insurance companies such as BUPA and PPP. Medical secretaries generally prepare and submit the claims and chase payment. Each medical secretary works for one or more (occasionally as many as 5) doctors. The top 1,000 claimants submit the majority of claims.

Insurers, doctors and patients all stand to gain if claims are validated at source and submitted electronically without involving the patients. The insurance companies devote considerable resources to claims processing and checking for possible abuse of the system. Doctors can be paid more quickly and with fewer queries. Removing them from the payment process reduces hassle to patients.

In 1995, BUPA and PPP (the two largest insurers) set up a Joint EDI (JEDI) project to submit claims from private hospitals via EDIFACT messages over a secure private network. This project was successful and over 150 hospitals are now submitting claims in this way. However, the EDIFACT software is complex to install and the private network fees are significant. In view of this, an alternative approach was developed, sending encrypted structured text messages over the Internet.

Most medical secretaries work independently using stand-alone PCs and they required an Internet connection (e-mail account) and appropriate encryption keys and certificates for sending and receiving encrypted email messages.

11.3 Method

The claims submission software uses Microsoft Outlook 98 as its foundation. Outlook is Microsoft's premier client for electronic messaging and workflow applications. Outlook 98 is the first Microsoft product to support S/MIME for sending encrypted electronic mail.

Custom contact forms were created for each patient, GP, healthcare professional, hospital and insurance company, based on the standard Outlook Contact form. These forms have been designed to meet the needs of medical secretaries. They include the data needed for claims submission as well as that needed for routine correspondence, including an interface to Microsoft Word. The digital certificates (including public keys) for users and insurance companies are held in the contact forms.

A special Claims Form was also written as a custom form, using a number of ActiveX components to find the patient and import fields from the patient form into the claim form, to validate the claim against insurance company rules and to encrypt the claim and submit it to the insurance company.

Each user requires an Internet email account. Getting connected to the Internet is not as simple as the advertisements would make it seem. We have reduced it to a 57-step process!

S/MIME is a specification for secure electronic messaging to prevent the interception and forgery of e-mail. S/MIME is short for Secure MIME, using Public Key Cryptography Standards (PKCS). Each participant needs a pair of cryptographic keys — a private key and a public key. The private key must be kept a tightly guarded secret, hidden in the computer, but the private key must be made known to all of the people with whom they wish to communicate using encrypted messages. A certification authority, such as VeriSign, certifies the authenticity of the public key.

The format for digital certificates is defined by the CCITT X.509 international standard; certificates can be read or written by any application complying with X.509. A digital certificate typically contains:

- Owner's public key
- Owner's name
- Expiration date of the public key
- Name of the issuer (the CA that issued the digital certificate)
- Serial number of the digital certificate
- Digital signature of the issuer

VeriSign digital certificates are available at three class levels, differentiated by the process used to verify the owner's identity. A Class 1 certificate verifies the owner's e-mail address, while a Class 2 involves additional verification of the owner's personal identity. The certificates normally expire after one year. This project used Class 1 certificates for the medical secretaries.

The number of secretaries, doctors, insurers and ISPs involved in the pilot project at October 1998 is shown in the next table:

Number of PCs (secretaries) connected	17
Number of Doctors involved	58
Number of Insurance Companies connected	2
Number of different ISPs used	8
Number of Claims submitted (April-October)	553

11.4 Discussion

Medical secretaries work on their own and can well be described as naïve users. They are highly dependent on their suppliers for installation and support. We had hoped to automate the process of Internet connection and application for digital certificates, but this has not proven easy to do.

The main reason why it has not proven possible to automate Internet connection and certificate applications is that the suppliers do not expose their object models to enable this to be done programmatically. In contrast we have been able to configure aspects of Outlook 98, which is superficially more complex, because Microsoft makes the full Outlook Object Model available to programmers.

The process of obtaining digital certificates from VeriSign is sensitive to the state of the machine when the keys are generated. For example, private keys generated while the PC is connected to a local area network (LAN) will not work when the machine is off-line.

Information service providers have significantly different protocols for connecting to the Internet. The procedure is complex. Demon Internet is currently the largest ISP in UK and has an advertising campaign using the slogans easy@pie and piece@cake. Respectfully we disagree. Users of corporate networks who have never tried to connect themselves to the Internet, should be aware that it is not entirely simple.

The precise mechanism of Secure MIME needs to be understood. When a message is encrypted, a one-off key is generated, known as the session key. This session key is used for symmetric encryption and decryption. The session key is encrypted to create two strings, first using the sender's public key and secondly by the recipient's public key. This means that both the sender and the receiver can decrypt the symmetric encryption key and hence read the original message.

Security in Outlook 98 cannot be implemented without at least one certificate being installed on the PC. It is possible to send encrypted mail, regardless of who is logged on to Windows, with any certificate installed, ie encrypted with the receiver's public key, but such mail cannot be re-opened in the sent mail folder unless the certificate owner is logged on to Windows.

Multiple keys can be installed for one Windows login. Users can select one for each Outlook profile and different keys for the purposes of encryption and for digital signatures. The chosen security level of the certificate does not affect the portability of certificates.

User names created a number of problems because the users, medical secretaries, worked for one or more doctors. The insurers consider that the doctors submit the claims. It is not practicable for one user to send encrypted messages on behalf of another. When creating encryption keys and certificates the name on the certificate must be the same as the Windows' logon name. A digital certificate can only be used within the Windows logon it was installed from.

11.5 Conclusions

This project involved a somewhat steeper learning curve than we anticipated at the outset. The main difficulties involved configuration and programming of Outlook 98, configuration of user systems for use with different ISPs, and misunderstanding the need for consistent user names on encryption certificates.

Once installed correctly, systems have run well with little need for day to day support.

For more information:
Tim Benson and Electronic Point of Care
E-mail: tbenson@epoc.co.uk

12. Summary of Described Security Problems and Solutions

Gunnar O. Klein

This volume provides a number of interesting examples of the security challenges facing health care organisations embarking on wide scale regional networking activities. It must be stressed that it is of course not the building of the physical and logical infrastructure as such that creates the main security requirements, it is the health telematics applications that provide the problems to solve.

The contributions herein describe the following main application security concerns:

Secure EDI

There will be for many years a strong need to protect messages sent by store and forward services encoded in Edifact, other non standard syntax or in the future soon in XML. These messages require the following type of security functions:

Data integrity and data origin authentication. These can both be readily solved by a digital signature mechanism as described in several contributions herein. One remaining difficulty is to find a standard way of signing different parts of a message. Current intersector standards only provide for one signature per message but this is the main requirement in most healthcare situations.

Data confidentiality of the message in transfer. The use of an hybrid encryption system combining a public key system for key exchange with a symmetric data encryption algorithm using a random session key is described in eg. The CoCo guidelines.

Accountability additional information. In addition to the above core services it is important to provide mechanisms to ensure accountability of various steps of the communication chain e.g. by audit logs but also in many cases to get a digitally signed proof of receipt of the intended recipient. This is a message protocol issue and does not invoke any special security mechanism other than a digital signature mechanism.

Access control

In all health information systems it is critical to be able to assess the authenticated secure user identity for access control purposes. It is described e.g. in the report from the Danderyd Hospital how one system allowing single sign on was installed in a complex network with many servers for complete medical records or for administrative tasks such as patient admission. Access control based on password authentication becomes very difficult to administer and is insecure in any large network also within an institution. When requiring access to different servers maintained in different locations and by different healthcare organisations of a region the new techniques with public key challenge response authentication using smart cards become very interesting as a secure and convenient solution.

The first problem with access control is to establish the authenticated identity of the person that wants to log on. The second important issue is to administer in a secure way how *authorisations* granting different types of rights, e.g. to read confidential information of a certain class, can be managed in a complex healthcare network. Within an institution, also a very large hospital, common authorisation servers that communicate with all the data servers using a cryptographically secure protocol are important tools. In this area there is little available in the form of formal standards but this volume contains examples of how this can be implemented using the Sesame concept as in the Star project or with the DHE platform in the HISA middleware solution described in chapter 9.

Protection of Data channels for on-line

Another common security demand in many healthcare applications is the need for a protection using both confidentiality encryption and mutual authentication in various direct communication scenarios. This is an important aspect of typical client-server applications like health record systems or today more and more in Web based applications. The report in chapter 8 on the Diabetes project T-IDDM is one interesting example of such security enhancements to the HTTP protocol. In the Internet world the SSL (Secure Socket Layer) protocol seems to have rapidly gained wide acceptance in providing some sort of basic necessary functionality.

Creating a structure of interoperative software components

There is a lot of interest these days for object oriented solutions using Corba or Microsoft COM/DCOM syntax. The idea of allowing software components to interact over inherently insecure networks is indeed challenging but is being addressed. In addition to the technical problems of using cryptographic techniques to secure the communication, the issue of administering the component authorisations is a formidable task in a complex multi-organisational network.

While many important approaches have been demonstrated here to solve some of the key issues it must also be stated that experiences of using these advance techniques are still rather limited.

13. Recommendations from SIREN

Security problems should no longer be regarded as absolute obstacles to the use of health telematics in large scale networking environments in a complete healthcare region or even nationally. There are a number of techniques available based on cryptographic principles that have been tested in practice that can provide adequate protection. The interoperabilty of all healthcare systems is a difficult goal and requires co-ordinated action. The objective of securing health telematics across borders at least within the European Union, may need further developments of standards, common legislation in key areas (including the restrictions on export and the use of cryptographic techniques in some member states) and the establishment of a network of co-operating Trusted Third Party Services which may need a common control framework.

The following recommendations are intended to guide the current mainly national regional health networks:

1. A public key cryptographic infrastructure (a PKI) should be established to support the following core security services:

- Secure user authentication
- Digital signatures for non repudiation
- Key Exchange for confidentiality encryption

2. An algorithm must be selected and the recommendation is to use RSA for all the above services. This selection is today very easy to make. It is the standard for Digital signatures in health care (ENV 12388) and there are lots of experiences as reported in this volume, there are many good reasons and products available to use it also for User Authentication and for Key Exchange.

3. Certification Service Providers (also called Certification Authorities) **must be established** that can receive the required trust and legal recognition within the intended area of communication. Even if there are in the public domain several Certification Policies (and Certification Practice Statements based on these) healthcare organisations in a region or country must get together and agree to use one of these. It may also be necessary for the healthcare organisations to invest or otherwise arrange for the establishment of such Certification Services to be provided in an effective and cost efficient way.

4. An infrastucture of directory services according to X.509 **should be established** to support access to public key certificates and, very importantly, to current information on possible revocations of issued certificates. Directories may be operated by Certificate issuers but could also be duplicated in systems operated by other structures such as one or more healthcare organisations in co-operation. An important reason for healthcare organisations to be involved in Directory services is that they can be very useful in a variety of ways for health care communication in addition to providing important services for a basic public key infrastructure.
Examples are:

Examples are:

- Providing access to contact information (name, address, telephone, e-mail, web address etc) of all healthcare organisations, units and professionals.
- Providing access to information on the provided services of the above including "EDI profiles".
- As a common distribution means for information on professional registrations preferably in the form of digitally signed certificates including the qualifications registered by a national or regional bodies such as a physician chamber or National board of health and welfare.
- Providing access to authorisations to information systems issued dynamically be various administrators of healthcare systems.

5. The use of smart cards is recommended for managing the core cryptographic functions linked to persons, professionals and in the future more and more also patients. The introduction of smart cards for security of health care systems used by professionals is on its way in several member states. The main function of the smart cards are to protect the private keys while providing an easy-to-use tool to bring them to any information system including the home PC where a healthcare professional needs to work. The Smart card issuing must be tightly linked to the Certification Service Providers and the certification policy should describe how cards are issued and used to protect the private keys corresponding to the public keys of the certificates. It should be recognised that the use of smart cards in a public key infrastructure is an area where Europe is in the lead compared to the US and where procurers of products for cryptographic support and certification services must be aware of the possible shortcomings of available US products. It can be recommended to carefully investigate European suppliers of security support products to US network application software including web browsers.

6. For efficient protection of confidentiality of data objects for communication in messaging or for direct data channel protection such as for a secure web access, **an hybrid encryption scheme is recommended** in addition to the public key infrastructure. This combines the use of the PKI for key exchange with the use of a more efficient symmetric algorithm. Currently only **triple DES and IDEA** can be recommended but may soon be complemented by the current US developments of a new Advanced Encryption Standard. The use of proprietary non-public algorithms (in some countries provided by national security agencies) for healthcare may be necessary but will always be expensive to use and prevent cross border communication.

7. Healthcare organisations should seek to use inter-sector, generic security solutions as much as possible. It should be emphasized that even if there are particularly strong requirements for security in healthcare and that there are some areas where healthcare specific problem arises, the main security requirements of networking in health is no different from that of other sectors. Therefore the use of protocols, products and services for general use should be preferred to special healthcare solutions whenever feasible. It is an important role however of healthcare actors to get together and select from among the available developments a set of security solutions that is suitable for the demands of the sector and inparticular for interoperability. A very important aspect of healthcare networking is the strong wish that any healthcare unit should be able to communicate with any other in a secure way at least within a region. The long term goal is to be able to provide seamless healthcare communication across Europe.

8. The use of formal European standards for appropriate security protocols should be encouraged. The European standardization organisation CEN with its technical committee TC 251 Health Informatics is very actively developing a series of standards to facilitate healthcare communication. The use of well established standards for the message constructions and basic terminology will not only be economically sound but will also help to avoid misinterpretation of the information transferred which might otherwise pose important threats to integrity and indirectly to the safety of the patient.
CEN/TC 251 also provides standards directly on security usually by providing a profile of some available international standard or other publicly available specification. The following documents can be recommended for use:

ENV 12388. *Medical Informatics — Algorithm for Digital Signature Services in Health Care*. This makes the well known RSA algorihtm mandatory.

ENV 12924. *Medical Informatics — Security Categorisation and Protection for Healthcare Information Systems*. This document provides a very useful guideline for assessing all aspects of necessary counter measures in order to protect different categories of health information systems.

Framework for Security of Healthcare Communication

This is a Technical Report due for publication in 1999 and available on the web-site below. This provides an overview of issues and an entry to the work of project team 39 mandated by EU and EFTA that will provide a three part standard on:

Security for Healthcare Communication:

Part 1. Concepts and Terminology
Part 2. Data Object Security
Part 3. Data Channel Security

Draft standards are available for public commenting from February 1999 on the TC 251 web server: www.centc251.org and the standards are due to be approved June 1999.

Another important standard under development is Secure User Identification — Strong Authentication using microprocessor cards developed by project team 37.

For the sharing and distribution of parts or complete healthcare records the developing standards for Electronic Healthcare Record Communication will be very important, particularly Part 3. Distribution rules which is available as a First working document from October 1998.

9. A number of European projects can provide important guidelines and provisional technical specifications for security of healthcare networks. The following can be listed in particular:

TrustHealth
SEMRIC
ISHTAR

10. The importance of non technical security policies and effective management must not be forgotten. A guideline can be found in ENV 12924 and the deliverables from the SEISMED health telematics project, see under bibliography below.

The secure communication of health information in regional networks is indeed a tremendous challenge. We have shown in this volume that today there are several powerful security techniques available to solve some of the key issues. It has been demonstrated here that the use of cryptographic techniques is indeed feasible and have been tested in various healthcare applications in different European countries.

We hope that the experiences presented herein and possible contacts for further details resulting from this book will be of assistance for those planning to set up a modern protection scheme for their health telematics applications. However, we would also like to emphasize that the large scale deployment of these protections mechnisms and a supporting infrastructure is by no means an easy task. The Siren team and its collaborating co-authors would very much welcome comments, questions and experiences on the issues presented here. The struggle for a better protection of patient related information must continue.

14. Authors

Editor

The main editor of this volume has been Dr **Gunnar O Klein** from the Centre for Health Telematics at the Karolinska Institute in Stockholm. Dr Klein who has been trained in both computer science and as a medical doctor, has been working only in informatics since 1985. Dr Klein has been the project manager of the SIREN accoumpanying measure as a consultancy assignment to Spri, the Swedish Institute for Health Services Development, the co-ordinating partner. Dr Klein was the project manager of the European projects Trustworthy Health Telematics (Infosec 1994) and of the TrustHealth 1 project, finalised 1997. In the follow up project TrustHealth 2 he is the technical co-ordinator.

Dr Klein has been active in standardisation formerly as the convenor of the European healthcare security working group but since 1997 he is the chairman of the parent committee, CEN/TC 251 Health Informatics. Dr Klein was recently appointed convenor of the newly established Security working group 4 of ISO/TC 215 Health Informatics. In Sweden he has been leading the national development (www.seis.se) towards the standardization of an Electronic Identity Card that was published as a national standard in September 1998.

Gunnar Klein
Centre for Health Telematics
Karolinska Institute
Jägargatan 20
177 77 Stockholm, Sweden
Tel.: +46 8 81 52 52
Fax: +46-8-449 03 52
E-mail: gunnar@klein.se

Chapter authors

Ricardo Bellazzi
Dipartimento di Informatica e Sistemistica
Universita' di Pavia
via Ferrata 1
27100 Pavia, Italy
Tel: +39-382-505-511
Fax: +39-382-505-373
E-mail: ric@ipvaimed3.unipv.it

Tim Benson
Chairman, Electronic Point of Care Ltd.
Trinity House, Heather Park Drive
Wembley, Middlesex, HA0 1SU, United Kingdom
Tel: +44-181 903 7060
E-mail: tbenson@epoc.co.uk

Bernd Blobel
Otto-von-Guericke University Magdeburg
Institute of Biometrics and Medical Informatics
Department of Medical Informatics
Leipziger Str. 44
D-39120 Magdeburg, Germany
Tel: +49-391-6713542
E-mail: Bernd.blobel@mrz.uni-magdeburg.de

Birgitta Wilson Claréus
Dept of Dermatology
Danderyd Hospital
E-mail: Birgitta.Clareus@hud.ds.sll.se

Paul Cooper
Project Manager Star & Intercare, IMS, Sandymount,
Station Road, Woburn Sands, MK17 8RR United Kingdom
Tel.: +44 1908 588806
E-mail: paul@mira.demon.co.uk

Fabrizio Massimo Ferrara
GESI Gestione Sistemi per l'Informatica srl & Consorzio EDITH
Via Rodi 32, 00195 Roma, Italy
Tel: +39 63 72 52 78
E-mail: fmf@gesi.it

Per Furberg
Associate Judge, Court of Appeal, Gothenburg
Pl 9208, 444 97 Svenshögen, Sweden
Tel.: +46+70 712 644
E-mail: per.furberg@mailbox,swipnet.se

Tor Olav Grotan
Senior consultant at KITH Norwegian centre for Medical Informatics
E-mail: tor.o.grotan@kith.no

C. Mossa
Dipartimento di Informatica e Sistemistica
Universita' di Pavia
via Ferrata 1, 27100 Pavia, Italy

Hubert Mensch
Actir-Santé S.A.
68 Route de Versailles Bâtiment 1C, BP 3
F-78430 Louveciennes, France
Tel.: +33-1-39.02.47.22
E-mail: hmensch@micronet.fr

Torleif Olhede
Director of Health Informatics at Spri
Box 70 487, S-107 26 Stockholm, Sweden
Tel.: +46-8-702 46 00.
E-mail: torleif.olhede@spri.se

Peter Pharow
Otto-von-Guericke University Magdeburg
Institute of Biometrics and Medical Informatics
Department of Medical Informatics
Leipziger Str. 44, D-39120 Magdeburg, Germany
Tel.: +49-391-6713543
E-mail: peter.pharow@mrz.uni-magdeburg.de

B. Riva
Dipartimento di Informatica e Sistemistica
Universita' di Pavia
via Ferrata 1, 27100 Pavia, Italy

Albert van der Werff
The SOCRATES Network
Vrouwgeestweg 20, 2481 KN Woubrugge, The Netherlands
Tel.: + 31 172 518910
E-mail: avdwsocr@wxs.nl

15. Bibliography

This is a list of selected references mentioned in the different chapters

European Union Directive 95/46/EC, On the Protection of Individuals with Regard to the Processing of Personal Data and on the Free Movement of such Data, OJ L281/31 - 50, 24 October 1995.

Council of Europe Recommendation, R(97)5, on The Protection of Medical Data, Council of Europe, Strasbourg, 13 February 1997.

European Commission: Proposal for a European Parliament and Council Directive on a common framework for electronic signatures COM (1998) 297 final, Brussels, 13 May 1998.

Proposal for a European Parliament and Council Directive on certain legal aspects of electronic commerce in the internal market. COM (1998), Brussels 23 December 1998.

Trusted Health Information Systems. A project within the DGXIII INFOSEC programme on Electronic signatures and trusted third party services. The following reports are available from Spri: Final deliverable part 1. Requirements on electronic signature services. Version 2, January 1995, Final deliverable part 2. Trusted Third Party Services. Version 2 January 1995, Trusted Health Information Systems Management Summary Brochure, December 1994.

TrustHealth 1 project : (Deliverable D6.2) Data Protection in Health Telematics Projects — Compliance with the European Directive on the Protection of Medical Data. (Sophie Louveaux and Yves Poullet, Centre de Recherches Informatique et Droit (C.R.I.D.), University of Namur.).

TrustHealth 1 project : (Deliverable D4.1) Functional Specification of TTP Services. Version 1.0.

TrustHealth 1 project : (Deliverable D4.2) Interface Specification of TTP Services. Version 1.0.

TrustHealth 1, Project HC1051, Deliverable D2.1, Selection of Security Services, 29 07 96, SPRI.

National Health Service Executive : Code of Connection for NHS organisations, IMG E5222.

International Journal of Biomedical Computing 43 (1996), pp 83-91: Sociotechnical aspects of the use of health related personal information for management and research. Kenneth R. Iversen and Tor Olav Grøtan, Norwegian Centre for Medical Informatics (KITH).

Blobel, B. (1996b) A Regional Clinical Cancer Documentation System for an Optimal Shared Healthcare in Cancer. In: J. Brender, J.P. Christensen, J.-R. Scherrer and P. McNair (edrs) Medical Informatics Europe '96, pp 1019-1026. IOS Press, Amsterdam.

Blobel, B. (1997b) Security Requirements and Solutions in Distributed Electronic Health Records. In: L.Yngström and J.Carlsen(edrs.) Information Security in Research and Business, pp 377-390. Chapman & Hall, London.

Blobel, B., Bleumer, G., Müller, A., Flikkenschild, E. and Ottes, F. (1997) Current Security Issues Faced by Healthcare Establishments. Deliverable of the HC1028 Telematics Project ISHTAR, February 1997.

Blobel, B, and Holena, M. (1997a) Comparing middleware concepts for advanced healthcare system architectures. International Journal of Medical Informatics 46 (1997) pp. 69-85.

Blobel, B. and Holena, M. (1997b) Security Threats and Solutions in Distributed, Interoperable Health Information Systems Using Middleware. In: J. Dudeck, B. Blobel, W. Lordieck and T. Bürkle (edrs.) New Technologies in Hospital Information Systems, pp. 66-73. IOS Press, Amsterdam.

The SEISMED Consortium (edr.) (1996) Data Security for Healthcare, Volume I-III. IOS Press, Amsterdam.

CEN/TC251 ENV 12967-1 'Health care Information Systems Architecture'.

The DHE middleware: - Information view, Functional view and API's — SPRI 1998.

A. Bakker, et al. International Journal of Medical Informatics, Special Issue Common Security problems for communicating patient data. Vol.49, No. 1, March 1998.

F.M. Ferrara, 'The management of authorisations and security in health care information systems', in 'Towards security in medical telematics', IOS Press, 1995.

G. Klein et al. "Trusted Health Information Systems", SPRI, Infosec-94 programme, Stockholm 1994.

Medical Informatics - Secure User Authentication for Health Care: management and Security of Authentication by Passwords, TC251 WG6, ref N95-022 rev, draft prENV, June 1995, CEN, Brussels, 1996 available on www.centc251.org.

ENV 12924: 1997. Medical Informatics - Security Categorisation and Protection for Healthcare Information

Systems. Available from National standards bodies or www.centc251.org.

ENV12388 (1997). Medical Informatics - Algorithm for Digital Signature Services in Healthcare, Available from National standards bodies or www.centc251.org.

Data Security for Health Care ed. the SEISMED Consortium, volumes in Studies in Health Technology and Informatics, IOS Press, Amsterdam, 1996. Vol. I Management Guidelines ISBN 90 5199 264 5 (series vol. 31) Vol. II Technical Guidelines, ISBN 90 5199 265 3 (series vol. 32) Vol. III User Guidelines, ISBN 90 5199 266 1 (series vol. 33).

Caring for Health Information: Safety, Security and Secrecy, ed Barber et al, pub for MA WG4 Elsevier, Amsterdam, ISSN 0020-7 1 01 [also in International Journal of Bio-Medical Computing, vol 35, Supplement February 1994].

Communicating Health Information in an Insecure World, ed Bakker AR et al, pub for RHA WG4 Elsevier, Amsterdam, 1996 IS SN 0020-7 1 01 [also in International Journal of Bio-Medical Computing, vol 43, Supplement October 1996].

Towards Security in Medical Telematics, ed Barber B et al, vol 27 in Studies in Health Technology and Informatics, IOS Press, Amsterdam, ISBN 90 5199 246 7.

16. Websites

16.1 European Commission

DG XIII's Information Servers:

I*M EUROPE: **www.echo.lu** Information about Europe and the European electronic information market. Direct access to ECHO, EC host offering free access to more than 20 online databases.

CORDIS: **www.cordis.lu** (Community R&D Information Service). Information on all EU-supported R&D activities including Programmes, Projects, Results, Publications and Partners.

ISPO: **www.ispo.cec.be** (Information Society Project Office). Information on Information Society activities.

Electronic Commerce related information from the Commission:

www.ispo.cec.be/ecommerce

where there are specific links into:

data protection:	**www.ispo.cec.be/ecommerce/dataprotect.htm**
security:	**www.ispo.cec.be/ecommerce/security1.htm**
issues:	**www.ispo.cec.be/ecommerce/issues.htm**
legal matters:	**www.ispo.cec.be/ecommerce/legal.htm**
projects:	**www.ispo.cec.be/ecommerce/projects.htm**

The draft digital signature directive:

europa.eu.int/comm/dg15/en/media/infso/sign.htm

16.2 European Health Telematics programme

An overview to all of the programme activitities can be found at

European Health Telematics Observatory

www.ehto.be or **www.ehto.org**

An Overview Of Issues in Health Data Security and Confidentiality Under the New European Data Protection Legislation. (Dr Petra Wilson, Visiting Scientist, Health Telematics, European Commission)

www.ehto.org/legal/data_confidentiality_security.html

The TrustHealth project:

www.ehto/projects/trusthealth

The Siren project

www.ehto/projects/siren

The CoCo project:

www.teb.upm.es/coco/coco.html

The Hansa project:

www.effdue.com/hansa

The SEMRIC project:

www.ehto.be/projects/semric

The Medsec project

www.math.aegean.gr/English/Academics/Research/Dfjrg/projects/medsec.htm

The Ishtar project

http://ted.see.plym.ac.uk/ishtar/

or

www.medicon.cz/Medicon/Project/Ishtar/Ishtar.html

16.3 Standardization

CEN/TC 251 European Committee for Standardization — Technical Committee 251 on Health Informatics.
Draft standards available on the web.

www.centc251.org

OII — European Commission Open Information Interchange
Information on virtually all ICT standards including Security

www2.echo.lu/oii/en/oiistand.html

ISO/TC 215/WG 4 Security of Health Informatics

www.hss.se/wg4.isotc215

16.4 National intitiatives

NHS UK

The National Health Service in UK has been active in the security area through the Security and Data Protection Programme which can be accessed from the NHS IMT home pages

www.imt4nhs.exec.nhs.uk

SEIS

Secure Electronic Information in Society, Sweden has a lot of information on the use of cryptographic techniques and electronic identity cards.

www.seis.se

Author Index